Attention

This book makes a valuable addition to the literature on attention. It is clearly written and conveys the growing interest in the neuropsychology of attention in an approachable and welcoming style.
Elizabeth Styles, Buckinghamshire Chilterns University College

Attention: A Neuropsychological Approach provides a fascinating overview of the neuropsychological aspects of attention, revealing how we select our information, divide our attention and control our focus of interest. Through fully integrating cognitive and neuropsychological perspectives on attention, Antony Ward demonstrates how each approach can illuminate the other. Examples are provided to show how the application of theories of attention can help to further our understanding of conditions such as dementia, schizophrenia, head injury and attention deficit hyperactivity disorder. This clear introduction will be of great interest to undergraduates studying neuropsychology, clinical psychology, occupational therapy and mental health nursing.

Antony Ward is head of Psychology at Newman College in Birmingham and has published numerous papers and a leading test battery for the assessment of attention.

Psychology Focus

Series editor: Perry Hinton, Oxford Brookes University

The Psychology Focus series provides students with a new focus on key topic areas in psychology. It supports students taking modules in psychology, whether for a psychology degree or a combined programme, and those renewing their qualification in a related discipline. Each short book:

■ presents clear, in-depth coverage of a discrete area with many applied examples
■ assumes no prior knowledge of psychology
■ has been written by an experienced teacher
■ has chapter summaries, annotated further reading and a glossary of key terms.

Also available in this series:

Friendship in Childhood and Adolescence
Phil Erwin

Gender and Social Psychology
Viv Burr

Jobs, Technology and People
Nik Chmiel

Learning and Studying
James Hartley

Personality: A Cognitive Approach
Jo Brunas-Wagstaff

Intelligence and Abilities
Colin Cooper

Stress, Cognition and Health
Tony Cassidy

The Social Psychology of Behaviour in Small Groups
Donald C. Pennington

Types of Thinking
Ian Robertson

Psychobiology of Human Motivation
Hugh Wagner

Stereotypes, Cognition and Culture
Perry R. Hinton

Psychology and "Human Nature"
Peter Ashworth

Abnormal Psychology
Alan Carr

Attitudes and Persuasion
Phil Erwin

The Person in Social Psychology
Viv Burr

Introducing Neuropsychology
John Stirling

Attention

A Neuropsychological Approach

■ Antony Ward

Ψ Psychology Press
Taylor & Francis Group

HOVE AND NEW YORK

First published 2004
by Psychology Press
27 Church Road, Hove, East Sussex
BN3 2FA

Simultaneously published in the
USA and Canada
by Psychology Press Inc
270 Madison Avenue, New York,
NY 10016

Typeset in Sabon by RefineCatch Ltd,
Bungay, Suffolk
Printed and bound in Great Britain by
TJ International Ltd, Padstow, Cornwall
Paperback cover design by Terry Foley

This publication has been produced
with paper manufactured to strict
environmental standards and with pulp
derived from sustainable forests.

*British Library Cataloguing in
Publication Data*
A catalogue record for this book is
available from the British Library

*Library of Congress Cataloging-in-
Publication Data*
Ward, Antony B.
    Attention : a neuropsychological
approach / Tony Ward – 1st ed.
        p. cm.
    Includes bibliographical references
and index.
    ISBN 1-84169-327-8 (hbk) – ISBN
1-84169-328-6 (pbk)
    1. Clinical neuropsychology. 2.
Attention. 3. Neuropsychological
tests. 4. Brain damage – Diagnosis.
I. Title.

    RC386.6.N48W374 2004
    616.8 – dc22
                                    2004006960

ISBN 1-84169-327-8 (hbk)

ISBN 1-84169-328-6 (pbk)

To Anna-Corinne and Amy-Rose

Contents

List of Illustrations

Series preface

The Psychology Focus series provides short, up-to-date accounts of key areas in psychology without assuming the reader's prior knowledge in the subject. Psychology is often a favoured subject area for study, since it is relevant to a wide range of disciplines such as Sociology, Education, Nursing, and Business Studies. These relatively inexpensive but focused short texts combine sufficient detail for psychology specialists with sufficient clarity for non-specialists. The series authors are academics experienced in undergraduate teaching as well as research. Each takes a topic within his or her area of psychological expertise and presents a short review, highlighting important themes, and including both theory and research findings. Each aspect of the topic is clearly explained with supporting glossaries to elucidate technical terms. The series has been conceived within the context of the increasing modularisation that has been developed in higher education over the last decade and fulfils the consequent need for clear, focused, topic-based course material. Instead of following one course of study, students on a modularization programme are often able to choose modules from a wide range of disciplines to complement the modules they are required to study for a specific degree. It can no longer be assumed that students studying a particular module will necessarily have the same background knowledge (or lack of it!) in that subject. But they will need to familiarize themselves with a particular topic rapidly as a single module in a single topic may be only 15 weeks long, with assessments arising during that period. They may have to combine eight or more modules in a single year to obtain a degree at the end of their programme of study. One possible problem with studying a range of separate modules is that the relevance of a particular topic or the relationship between topics might not always be apparent. In the Psychology Focus series, authors have drawn where possible on practical and applied examples to support the points being made so that readers can see the wider relevance of the topic under study. Also, the study of psychology is usually broken up into separate areas, such as social psychology, developmental psychology, and cognitive psychology, to take three examples. While the books in the Psychology Focus series will provide excellent coverage of certain key topics within these "traditional" areas, the authors have not been constrained in their examples and explanations and may draw on material across the whole field of psychology to help explain the topic under study more fully. Each text in the series provides the reader with a range of important material on a specific topic. They are suitably comprehensive and give a clear account of the important issues involved. The authors analyse and interpret the material as well as present an up-to-date and detailed review of key work. Recent references are provided along with suggested further reading to allow readers to investigate the topic in more depth. It is hoped, therefore, that after following the informative review of a key topic in a Psychology Focus text, readers not only will have a clear understanding of the issues in question but will be intrigued and challenged to investigate the topic further.

Preface

When I was studying for my undergraduate degree in psychology at the University of Hertfordshire in the early 1980s, I remember that, of all the areas of cognitive psychology, attention was for me probably the least inspiring. Avenues of research begun in the 1950s and 1960s seemed to have petered out in a dead end, with much energy expended over the issue of early versus late selection. At times these theoretical arguments seem to revolve around very subtle distinctions indeed.

However, my interest in the topic revived while in the later stages of my PhD at Guy's Hospital. My remit was to explore ways of assessing patients with advanced dementia, as part of a large multidisciplinary study into the neurochemical basis of Alzheimer's disease. Initially, it seemed my efforts would revolve around behavioural observation techniques but as the work progressed my efforts turned towards looking at residual cognitive abilities, using a structured interview. It quickly became apparent that what we were really measuring using this technique was the patients' ability to attend and remain oriented to their environment. The direct relevance of attentional theory to this clinical situation revived my interest in the topic and I went looking for the relevant literature. To my surprise, there was virtually no literature on attention in dementia at that time. [See, for example, Hart and Semple (1990) where attention warrants a few pages in the whole of a book devoted to the neuropsychology of the dementias.]

I was pleased, therefore, when, on finishing my PhD, I was offered the opportunity to work with Ian Robertson at the MRC Applied Psychology Unit in Cambridge. My major task over the following 2 years was to develop the Test of Everyday Attention, a comprehensive, theoretically inspired battery for the assessment of this important domain. I knew from my own experience that it was much needed.

In subsequent years my interest has never wandered far from the topic of attention and much of my efforts have been directed to the issue of executive function and attentional control. In the mid-1990s I spent some time working out how control functions could be explained from a neural network perspective, and some of my current work looks at the role of language as a mediator of control.

This book, then, is a product of my ongoing reflections on the subject of attention over the last decade and a half. It has been an exciting period, with much renewed interest and efforts in previously unexplored areas. For example, the issue of attention in dementia has at last achieved the prominence it deserves. I have no doubts that should I come to revise this book after a similar lapse of time, the field will have moved on by at least as much again. I therefore thoroughly recommend the topic, both as an important issue within cognitive psychology and as a potentially rewarding subject of study to future researchers.

My aim in writing the book is to show readers how theories of attention devised by cognitive psychologists can be useful in helping us to understand the effects of brain damage on patients. At the same time, the insights gained from working with and studying patients can often serve to validate theories of normal cognition. To the extent that the reader is finally able to appreciate these two points, I will have succeeded. On the other hand, the book does not set out to be a comprehensive account of either cognitive theories or findings from neuroscience. Such accounts can be found elsewhere. It is my hope that the book will have wide appeal. Undergraduate psychology students will find it interesting in that they will see how the dry and technical theories of attention can be useful in applied contexts. The book will therefore serve as useful supplementary reading alongside traditional accounts of cognitive psychology. Students of clinical psychology will be interested to learn of how attention is affected in the variety of clinical conditions considered. Finally, researchers on the neuropsychology of attention may find it useful to have summaries of research on topics outside of their immediate current concerns.

To some extent I have tried to make the theoretical chapters (i.e. Chapters 4–7) free standing. This is so that they can be used in isolation, thus someone wanting an account of findings on selective attention can read Chapter 5 without having to read Chapter 4. This means there is a slight amount of repetition, in particular where certain tests are mentioned several times and details of their administration are necessary to understanding the material. However, I have tried to keep this to a minimum, and this is further served by the inclusion of Chapter 3, which describes the most important tests used in this domain in clinical practice. Most readers will therefore wish to ensure that they are familiar with Chapter 3 before moving on to the theoretical chapters, and readers will wish to refer back to this chapter as necessary.

Finally, I should point out that this book was substantially written between the summer of 2002 and the spring of 2003, during which time I was a senior lecturer at the University of the West Indies in Kingston, Jamaica. This will explain the occasional references to Caribbean phenomena and experiences. I am indebted to my students at that time, who were exposed to draft forms of much of the material.

I would like to thank Nick Lund and Liz Styles for their helpful review of the manuscript, and a further anonymous reviewer without whose diligence and painstaking efforts the book would not be what it is today.

Tony Ward
March 2003

Chapter 1

What is attention?

Everyone knows what attention is. It is the taking possession of the mind, in clear and vivid form, of one out of what seemed several simultaneously possible objects or trains of thought. Focalization, concentration, of consciousness are of its essence.

—William James (1890)

Overview

THIS CHAPTER COMMENCES with a brief introduction to the topic of attention. It then goes on to introduce the relevant cognitive theories to the reader (or revise the concepts for those who have previously studied the subject). These theories will recur as subsequent chapters describe how they have guided research with various types of patients. Clearly, then, a good grasp of the material in this chapter will be essential to fully appreciating that presented in later chapters. Readers who are familiar with the various theories may choose to skip this chapter or concentrate on those sections that deal with unfamiliar material.

Introduction

Our ability as human beings to selectively focus our attention on specific features of our environment is undoubtedly of fundamental importance in allowing us to adapt to an ever more complex and richer world. Take a common experience, such as standing on the concourse of a major railway station or airport, and imagine all the sights and sounds bombarding your senses and demanding recognition. Were you not able to screen out some of this abundance of stimuli, then such an experience would be daunting indeed. The study of these key mental processes has become the concern of a major strand of modern psychology, the study of cognition. This area of psychology has been a major part of the discipline for over 40 years and, from the outset, the study of attention has been an important element, for example with the publication of a highly influential work by Broadbent in 1958. Since that time, psychologists have sought to take real-world problems, such as how we deal with several sounds simultaneously, and study them in the laboratory under carefully controlled conditions.

Over the last few decades many hundreds if not thousands of such studies have focused upon the topic of attention, looking at the phenomenon from many different angles. The observations and data gathered have led to a number of theories explaining how humans attend to their environment. More recently, clinical psychologists have come to realize that these cognitive theories can provide a very useful framework for understanding the problems of their patients. At the same time, cognitive psychologists have come to see that observing the difficulties experienced by patients with certain conditions can be a useful source of additional data. This evidence can serve to confirm or discredit those theories, often provoking revision and reconsideration. This synergy between basic laboratory-based research and clinical work with patients has in recent times led to additional interest in the area of cognitive science. The joint efforts of neuroscientists and cognitive psychologists are now seen as indispensable to a fuller understanding of the human brain. The aim of this book is to illustrate for the reader how this process has enhanced our understanding of attention and its disorders. Twenty years ago a book on cognitive neuropsychology (the application of cognitive theories to neurological disorders) would have been difficult to write, since the approach was in its infancy. Ten years ago, such a book focusing on attention would have been just as difficult to conceive, since the early neuropsychological research tended to focus on memory and language. It is interesting to note, for example, that an important text on the neuropsychology of dementia, published just over a decade ago (Hart & Semple, 1990), contained only a very modest section on attention. In the last 10 years this situation has changed dramatically. Many neuropsychologists realized that the lack of research on attention represented a major omission from the knowledge base. Further, many suspected that attentional processes were really at the core of difficulties experienced by many patients, which were being described as memory or other deficits. For example, we now know that patients with Alzheimer's disease often exhibit severe attentional difficulties in the early stages of the disorder, often before symptoms have manifested themselves in other areas (e.g. Parasuraman & Haxby, 1993).

As a result of this increased interest in the topic, it is now possible to consider the neuropsychology of attention as an area in its own right, and this book sets out to introduce readers to this domain. Given its youth, there is no doubt that this area of work will experience considerable progress in the years ahead. Should any of the readers of this book come to be involved in that endeavour, having been inspired by these pages, then it will have admirably served its purpose. It is also the author's hope that this introduction to the neuropsychology of attention will prove useful to clinicians working with the various types of patient who suffer from the disorders that will be considered.

What is attention?

Cognitive theories of attention can seem very complex and abstract. In reality, these theories are trying to describe quite simple aspects of behaviour that we can all understand. To help the reader, therefore, each of the following sections briefly considers everyday examples of behaviour, which are thought to involve the aspects of attention being described. Subsequently, the theoretical accounts psychologists have given for those behaviours will be reviewed. The various theories of attention can be covered under the headings of selection, dividing attention, control, and vigilance.

Selective attention

The quote given at the start of this chapter seems to have become de rigueur as a way of opening discussions such as this on the nature of attention. James' view is that the term "attention" refers to the process by which we are able to focus on a particular aspect of our environment. Thus that aspect becomes the only thing we are aware of at that particular moment in time. Probably one of the best examples of this in the modern world is the experience of watching television. When we are engrossed in a favourite television programme we may be unaware of other things happening in the room around us. We may not hear someone in the room asking us a question, or may be unaware of events taking place outside. However, at any given time we can change the focus of our attention. As James pointed out, our own trains of thought may distract us, causing us to shift our focus, perhaps gazing out of a window to see if it has started to rain, or listening intently to hear if the washing machine has stopped. In a modern home there are many such distractions, leading us to take precautions when we are especially keen to concentrate on something, e.g. by unplugging the phone. The cinema is the classic example of distraction management, leading many of us to emerge blinking after 2 hours of total immersion from a world of undistracted movie fantasy. This may be the reason why cinemas remain popular in this era of unlimited home entertainment.

The modern phenomena of television is an example of a multi-sensory stimulus capable of holding our attention for considerable periods of time, but we could cite simpler examples of focused attention that use a single sense. For example, a street map is a simple device that allows any of us to pinpoint an unfamiliar location in unknown territory. To use it, we have to look up in the index a grid reference for the street we want to find and then scan that grid of the map for our location. In this example, the focus of our attention is visual. A similar experience is scanning a telephone directory for a particular name. In both examples we are focusing our vision on a particular location, and trying to select a particular stimulus from a range of items. Imagine if the telephone directory was particularly large, or the street map especially dense. What would determine how successful we were in our task, i.e. how quickly we could find the desired name or street? Clearly we would need to stay very focused on the directory or map, not allowing ourselves to be distracted. Imagine carrying out such a task in a quiet room at home compared to a busy shopping centre or on a busy main road. Also, we would need to concentrate on finding the particular name or street, not being distracted by other items on the map or names in the directory. It also helps that modern maps tend to use a variety of very different symbols to represent different types of land-based features.

Moving to an auditory example, we often find ourselves in a noisy environment, having to focus upon a particular stimuli while trying to ignore a multitude of competing sounds. Imagine, for example, trying to have a conversation in a busy café with many competing sounds going on around. Many of us will know how difficult it is to make phone calls from such difficult environments as railway station concourses. In such situations we have to concentrate on one particular conversation, while trying to ignore the sound of other voices competing for our attention. Many of us will also have had the experience of having a conversation with someone in which we have only a partial interest, and finding it very difficult to ignore a conversation going on nearby in which we have a much greater interest. Imagine, for example, that you are at a party and find yourself talking to someone about last weekend's football results, when you would be much more interested in talking about office politics and in fact someone nearby is discussing the latest list of office promotions and appointments. Under such circumstances many of us would find ourselves distracted by the conversation going on nearby, and perhaps even be embarrassed at the frequency with which we might find ourselves having to ask our footballing acquaintance to repeat crucial facts.

All of the above examples show how, in the real world, we often choose to focus on a particular stimuli, either auditory or visual. In fact if we reflect a little more, it is not that we *choose* to select, but rather that we are *forced* to, as we are not able to attend to everything at once; we can only focus on one conversation at a time. Even if we install two televisions in our lounge so as to be able to watch more of our favourite programmes, we will struggle to follow what is happening on them simultaneously. Provided we focus our attention on a single source of information, i.e. one television or one conversation, we are able to perform the task with relative ease, but at the expense of becoming less aware of other things going on around us.

These kinds of common-sense reflections are found in the earliest theories of attention. For example, Cherry (1953) studied the "cocktail party" phenomenon. This relates to the situation in which we are able to follow a single conversation even when there are many other conversations going on around us, the kind of situation we encounter at parties. To control this situation in the laboratory, Cherry devised the Dichotic Listening Test (Figure 1.1). This involves the independent playing of two messages through headphones, one to either ear. To

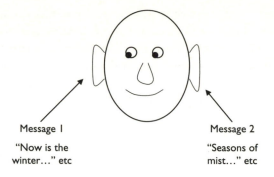

Message 1
"Now is the
winter..." etc

Message 2
"Seasons of
mist..." etc

Figure 1.1   **The dichotic listening task**
Two messages are played to the participant simultaneously, one to each ear.
The participant then has to repeat out loud one of the messages (shadow),
so he or she would say "now is the winter . . ." etc if asked to follow the right
ear.

ensure that participants attend fully to the voice in one ear, they are typically asked to *shadow* that message, i.e. to repeat it out loud. Sometimes the messages presented are text passages, sometimes they may be letter or number strings. So a participant may hear "now is the winter of our discontent . . ." Played to the right ear and "Remember thy creator in the time of thy youth . . ." played to the left. If they were asked to shadow the right then they would say out loud "now . . . is . . . the . . . winter . . ." and so on in synchrony with the recording. This is a very effective technique for ensuring that participants listen only to the message to be attended. The question then is, what if anything do they notice about the unattended message? The answer according to Cherry was remarkably little, other than the gross physical characteristics, e.g. the pitch and timbre of the voice. Participants could not recall anything of what was actually said, and frequently even failed to notice if the unattended message were being presented in a foreign language!

In his influential 1958 book, Broadbent theorized about the nature of these observations. He proposed that the human attentional system must have a limited capacity, since there is a very finite limit on how much information we can attend to at once. Further, since

7

this capacity can be applied to a wide variety of tasks and situations, e.g. reading a book, looking at a map, or holding a conversation, it must be general purpose. To protect this limited capacity, Broadbent proposed that our attentional system was set up to process one information source at a time, what he termed a "single channel". All other unattended channels would be filtered out, and this filtering was done based on gross physical characteristics (Figure 1.2). Thus the only thing that participants would be aware of in the unattended channel during the dichotic listening task would be the gross physical features. The theory could account for all the data collected at the time, and seemed a plausible account.

Within a few years, however, other workers were raising difficulties for Broadbent's account. One of Broadbent's former PhD students pointed out that sometimes information could intrude from the unattended channel (Treisman, 1960, 1964). For example, if participants were asked to tap each time they heard the word "tap" in the attended channel, then occasionally they would tap in response to the word being presented on the unattended channel. According to Broadbent's account this should not happen (although the possibility that participants might actively be shifting their attention during the task does not seem to have been adequately considered—see later). In another elegant experiment, Corteen and Dunn (1971) conditioned words to produce a galvanic skin response (GSR) response (a stress reaction based on increased perspiration) by being paired with a mild electric shock. They found that such words continued to elicit a GSR

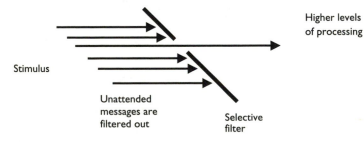

Figure 1.2 **Broadbent's filter model of attention**

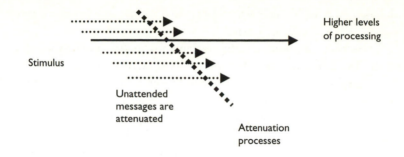

Stimulus

Higher levels
of processing

Unattended
messages are
attenuated

Attenuation
processes

Figure 1.3 **Treisman's model of attenuation**

even when presented in the unattended channel during a shadowing task. Treisman's solution to this difficulty was to propose a modification of Broadbent's theory, such that unattended information was not completely filtered out by the attentional system, instead it was "attenuated". Thus information from the unattended channel is not lost to higher processes, but it is not as readily available, in a sense it is "turned down" (Figure 1.3). An alternative and quite different view was put forward by Deutsch and Deutsch (1963), who suggested that no filtering or attenuation takes place, instead all inputs are fully processed and available. However, since unattended inputs are not selected for any further processing, they are very quickly lost. In this account information to be attended to is determined partly by "pertinence", i.e. its relevance to the current context and task demands (Figure 1.4). This can explain why a participant's name is frequently able to draw his or her attention when presented in the unattended

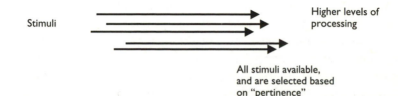

Stimuli

Higher levels of
processing

All stimuli available,
and are selected based
on "pertinence"

Figure 1.4 **Deutsch and Deutsch pertinence model**

channel. Such highly relevant and personal information as one's own name is always highly pertinent.

Because all inputs remain available for higher-order processing in the Deutsch and Deutsch theory it is sometimes referred to as a "late selection" account, whereas Broadbent's and Treisman's views are said to be "early selection". In time, Treisman's view came to prevail, with many current workers (e.g. Driver, 2001) suggesting that recent neurophysiological work supports the notion of early selection with attenuation. For example, Moran and Desimone (1985) describe how, in their animal research, covert attention strikingly modulates the degree to which a stimulus is represented in the visual cortex, with unattended stimuli being much less evident. In the Deutsch and Deutsch account we might have expected all stimuli to be strongly represented in the earlier processing stages, i.e. in the cortical areas serving early visual processes.

Although these studies have continued to be influential, there were at the time some significant criticisms of the methodologies used in this early line of research. For example, it was suggested that shadowing is a highly artificial task. Rarely in life do we repeat, parrot fashion, what someone is saying to us in a conversation. Moray (1959) showed that an experienced participant could easily cope with shadowing and successfully carry out other task demands, e.g. listening out for target words in the unattended channel. This led to a number of the original key studies being carried out without shadowing. Generally the results were much less dramatic, but still showed an advantage to the attended channel. Later, Moray (1969) showed that without the shadowing requirement, skilled participants could in fact attend to two simultaneous channels, and that this is achieved by rapidly switching back and forth from one channel to another. Moray suggested that the switch time was remarkably short, within the order of 25 ms. This realization that people could rapidly switch their attention from one source of information to another led to a dilemma that has never satisfactorily been resolved, and that might have contributed to researchers moving away from this particular research topic. The dilemma is that if information channels could be switched so rapidly then there is currently no satisfactory way of deciding whether attention consists of a single channel, which can be rapidly alternated across different sources, or of multiple sources of incoming information, which can genuinely be processed in parallel. In other words, Treisman's attenuated information in the unattended channel could result from people temporarily switching their attention from the attended channel during downtime, i.e. in the periods when active processing requirements have declined. For example, while listening to the attended message there may be gaps between words. Also, once the participant has identified the next word in the message he or she no longer has to fully attend to the ending of the word, particularly if it has been strongly cued by semantic association and context. If this suggestion was proved correct then Broadbent would have been right all along. Certainly, most people's day-to-day experience is that it is extremely difficult, if not impossible, to hold two simultaneous, fast-moving conversations.

In the 1970s, the focus of attentional researchers moved from the auditory to the visual domain, in part probably because visual attention is easier to study methodologically. For example, stimuli can be presented for precise amounts of time, with the stimulus onset being clearly identifiable (important when trying to measure reaction times). There are many parallels between the two domains but also some major differences. Like auditory stimuli, it was demonstrated in the 1960s that vision operates through a limited-capacity sensory buffer, called the iconic store. Thus if we briefly present participants with a 3 × 3 array of letters (see Figure 1.5) and ask them to recall them, they will manage only a few items.

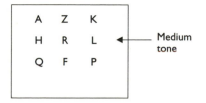

Figure 1.5 **Typical display used in iconic memory experiments**
A grid of nine letters is presented on the screen briefly. Recall of the whole grid is poor but if a particular row is indicated with either a high, medium, or low tone, then recall of that row is perfect.

If, however, we present a cue immediately after the grid and instruct the participants that they are to recall either the top, middle, or bottom row using a low, medium, or high tone, then recall of the required row is perfect. This indicates that for an instant of time after presentation, an image of the grid remains in the sensory buffer, and if the cue arrives in time then participants are able to direct their attention to the required row (Sperling, 1960). You should be able to observe this effect for yourself by staring at the example grid for a few seconds and then looking away. For a brief instant you should be able to observe an image of the grid in your "mind's eye". A similar store operates in the auditory domain and is called "echoic" memory.

As in the auditory domain, visual researchers have investigated the extent to which unattended stimuli are processed. For example, Rock and Gutman (1981) showed participants line drawings of objects superimposed on top of another. One object was drawn in red, the other in green. If participants are instructed to attend only to red-coloured objects, then their subsequent recall of green-coloured objects is very poor, a result similar to that found with the unattended auditory channel in the dichotic listening task. This would appear to suggest that the green objects have received little if any processing. However, subsequent studies refute this. For example, Tipper (1985) manipulated the relationship between the ignored stimuli on one trial and the to-be-attended stimuli on the next, such that they were semantic associates (i.e. objects that people typically associate with each other, such as knife and fork). For example, in one trial participants might have to name a picture of a bus while ignoring a fork, while on the next trial they have to name a knife and ignore a chair. Tipper found that where a to-be-ignored stimulus was related to a subsequent to-be-attended stimulus, that subsequent stimulus was processed more slowly than it would otherwise have been. Naming a knife when you have just ignored a fork is harder than if you had to name the knife after ignoring a neutral unrelated stimuli. This phenomenon is called negative priming, and it seems to imply that the ignored stimuli have in fact had some impact on the cognitive system since there is an effect on the subsequent trial (Figure 1.6). Thus it seems that in the visual field, unattended items are processed to some degree.

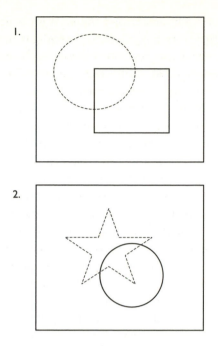

Figure 1.6 **Negative priming experiments**
Each box represents a trial in a negative priming experiment, where the task is to name the solid shape. In the second trial, the circle is likely to be named slower, since it was the to-be-ignored stimulus on the immediately preceding trial.

Unlike the auditory domain, visual attention involves scanning a well-defined area in terms of the visual field. Often, we direct our visual attention with eye movements, but we do not need to. It is possible to direct one's attention around the visual field while keeping the eyes fixated on a particular point. For example, we have probably all had the experience of observing something out of the corner of our eye. This is referred to as covert attention, and it is often described as being like a spotlight. In other words, the main focus of our attention covers a limited portion of the visual field, and this attentional hot spot can be moved around (Posner, 1980). In addition, the spot can vary in size, from small to large, and in this sense has been described as being like a zoom lens (although since spotlights can also be varied in size I have never really understood the need for a new metaphor to cover this property). As this attentional spotlight moves around the visual environment it engages with the various objects in the scene. Posner and Petersen (1990) outlined a number of putative processes engaged in the movement of spatial attention, including engaging, disengaging, and shifting. As we will see in Chapter 5, patients with various disorders of visual attention have been found to have problems with these separate processes, lending support to Posner and Petersen's formulation. It is worth considering briefly at this point the kinds of paradigms (i.e. experimental methods) that Posner and his colleagues have used (Figure 1.7). As we shall see, these methods have frequently been applied to patients. In a typical experiment, the participant focuses his or her vision on a central point on a screen, and shortly afterwards a target (e.g. a letter) is presented on either the right or left. This gives a measure of how quickly the participant is able to shift attention across to the target. In a classic sequence of early studies, it was found that if a central cue appears just before the target (a small arrow pointing left or right), then the target is detected faster. Note that this is despite the fact that there is not time for the person to redirect his or her gaze between the cue and the target appearing. People must therefore be able very quickly to redirect their attention covertly within the visual scene. Other studies have found that where a target is presented and remains on screen during presentation of a second target, some patients have trouble responding to the second target. It is as if their attention has been captured by the first stimulus, and they cannot disengage it to attend to the second target. As long as the first target disappears, thus freeing their attention, they are fine.

Often, when we move our visual attention we are looking for something in particular, and this situation has been subject to numerous laboratory studies. Typically, participants are presented with an array of stimuli and have to search for a particular stimulus type. For example, they may be looking for the letter "O" in an array of "X" distracters. In tasks such as this "pop-out" is typically observed, that is to say that the letter "O", being distinct from the distracters, is immediately obvious. Such a search is said to be fast because much of the stimulus processing occurs in parallel and it does not make much difference to the decision speed how many distracters

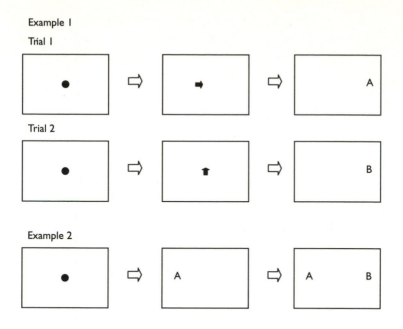

Figure 1.7 Illustration of the type of paradigm typically employed by Posner and colleagues

In example 1, trial 1, a central fixation point is followed by a cue, correctly pointing in the direction of the about to be presented target. The target is immediately presented. This can be contrasted with the situation shown in trial 2, where the cue is now neutral. A further manipulation is to have the cues misdirecting on some trials, i.e. pointing in the wrong direction.

In example 2, a target is presented on the left hand side, which remains on the screen when a second target appears on the right hand side. Some patients are unable to "disengage" from the first target.

there are. Contrast this with searching for an upside-down letter "T" among letter "L"s and letter "T"s in different orientations (see Figure 1.8). Now the task is much harder, and the search is said to be serial, i.e. each stimuli must be individually checked to see if it matches the conjunction of two features being searched for (letter "T", upside down). These observations were explained by Treisman (1988) in her Feature Integration Theory, which posits that features are processed very fast and in parallel, thus a search that can be conducted based on a single discriminating feature can be very fast, giving the appearance

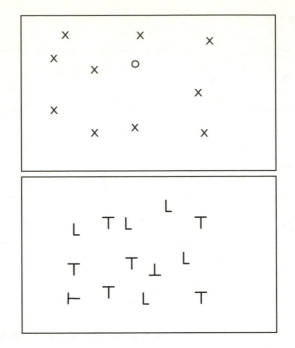

Figure 1.8 Visual search tasks

Compare searching for the letter "O" in the top box with an upside-down "T" in the box below. In the former case, pop-out occurs, because the letter "O" shares no features with the letter "X". In the latter, search is harder, since "L" and "T" share features, and to identify the upside-down "T" one has to check two features, shape and orientation.

of pop-out. Integration of features, however, involves location, and is serial. Thus when a visual search requires several features to be taken into account, the process is much slower. This account fits in with our current views of cortical processing, with some areas of visual cortex coding for specific features and others coding for location.

Going back to our everyday visual search example, it should now be clear that if we are looking for a particular feature on a map, the speed with which we will be able to find it will depend on how distinct the various symbols being used are. This, of course, is a problem with typical street maps, since all streets share similar features and little attempt is made to use colour or different fonts for different types of street, e.g. avenues, roads, closes. How much easier if roads were colour-coded according to size and street names are coded using different fonts; the usability would be far greater than currently tends to be the case.

In summary, it seems that when we attend closely to a stimulus, this precludes us having an in-depth awareness of simultaneous stimuli to which we are not actively attending. However, unattended stimuli are not completely unprocessed. There is good evidence from neurophysiology and the observed effects of unattended stimuli on subsequent trials that unattended stimuli are processed to some degree. Whether this continued availability of unattended stimuli is due to a mechanism such as attenuation, or perhaps from transient redirection of attention remains to be seen (although these two possibilities could be conceived as being functionally equivalent).

Divided attention

So far we have discussed the extent to which it is possible to selectively attend to information, and to what extent ignored stimuli are processed. In the real world, the demands made upon us often require that we try and attend to several stimuli at once, or even try and carry out two tasks simultaneously. In fact, this situation is common place, and we carry it out with varying degrees of success. The issue we are talking about is the extent to which we are able to divide our attention.

Driving a car is the classic example of a situation which requires us to divide our attention, and one that most adults are personally familiar with. It is a good example because it illustrates several theoretical issues which we will touch upon. Driving a car requires us to pay attention to multiple sources of information at once. As such, it represents a complex multitasking environment. For example, to drive a car along a road (assuming it has a manual gearbox) one has to pay careful attention to the road ahead and events developing along the side of the road. The steering wheel must be constantly adjusted to keep the vehicle moving along the required trajectory. One also has to pay attention to events happening behind the vehicle, requiring frequent glances at the rear view mirror. One must also glance from time to time at the speedometer, to ensure that one is sticking within the speed limit. In addition, a good driver is carefully monitoring the performance of the vehicle, listening to the engine and feeling how much throttle is being applied by the right foot, in order to decide whether the gear is appropriate or needs to be changed. If a gear change is called for then a whole sequence of additional demands arise, involving depressing the clutch and manipulating the gear lever. Similarly, reducing speed requires attention to the clutch and brake. Should it start raining, then one will have to attend to the windscreen wiper lever, and monitor the speed of the wipers to ensure that the selected speed matches the density of rainfall. Skilled drivers might be surprised to be reminded of all the intricate tasks they routinely accomplish when driving from A to B. To learner drivers, the whole thing initially seems quite daunting, as they struggle to accomplish all the tasks and perform them in the right sequence. Needless to say, listening to the car radio is not recommended for the novice driver, and yet very quickly we are able to listen to the radio, talk to a passenger, and accomplish the task of driving. So effortless does the task of driving become, that we can drive along on autopilot while our mind thinks of other things. Long distances can be covered with little recollection of what happened along the way. Yet sometimes we are reminded that driving can be demanding. When we have to negotiate a difficult intersection or drive in dense traffic, then we may struggle to keep up the conversation with our passenger or listen to the discussion programme taking place on the radio. Anyone who has tried to utilize their drive time more productively through the use of self-improvement audiotapes can tell you that there are times when you have to turn the tape off, and each year many accidents occur when people try to maintain a mobile phone conversation while driving in traffic. It is not surprising that the motor industry has tried to reduce the demands on the driver through the use of technology such as automatic trans- missions. Some cars are now even sensitive to the amount of rain fall, and automatically adjust the speed of the windscreen wipers to match, not to mention turning the lights on when it gets dark.

Given the scenario outlined above, the issues that have been of interest to psychologists should be fairly apparent. How many stimuli or tasks can a person successfully attend to at once? What are the characteristics of tasks that can be combined? For example, is it easier to combine an auditory and a visual task than, say, two auditory or two visual tasks? (we know from the work on selective attention that the shadowing technique virtually precludes participants from attending to a second auditory message) and what are the effects of practice? (again, we know from the work on selective attention that expert shadowers are able to listen to a second message).

Generally speaking, when people try to combine two tasks they are worse at performing them together than when they perform them alone. This is sometimes referred to as the dual task deficit. For example, Crook, West, and Larrabee (1993) showed that when a driving task was combined with other tasks, driving performance suffered, with the greatest changes in the young (18–35) and old (65+) age groups. This finding in respect to age probably reflects the fact that younger, less experienced drivers suffer greater interference from a distracter task, as do older drivers who have fever cognitive resources. Similarly, Strayer and Johnston (2001) showed that use of either a hand-held or hands-free mobile phone to hold an unrestrained conversation reduced driving performance. They were careful to narrow down the explanation by ruling out other factors, e.g. by having participants articulate a set phrase, or use a hand-held mobile phone in a tracking task. Thus driving performance will suffer if combined with other tasks, particularly if those competing tasks require a high degree of concentration, such as talking on a mobile phone.

Although any two tasks will interfere to some degree when combined, some tasks will interfere with each other more than others. One factor that appears to determine this is task similarity. Wickens (1984) reviewed this issue, and suggested that tasks will interfere if they use the same modality, require similar kinds of processing (e.g. two memory tasks), use the same internal codes (e.g. verbal or visual) or require similar types of response. Tasks will also interfere more if they are more demanding. For example, Bourke, Duncan, and Nimmo-Smith (1996) combined a variety of tasks that varied in complexity, showing that the more complex consistently interfered with the other tasks in the predicted direction. This was despite all the tasks used by Bourke et al. being very different in nature, e.g. random number generation combined with tone discrimination. These authors argue that their results support the notion of central capacity limitations in dual task interference, since it is hard to explain the consistency of their interference results in terms of task similarity. It is, however, difficult to define task demands, although Bourke (1997) has proposed one possible method.

People can perform two tasks better if they have been able to practice them, and this practice should ideally be in doing the combined tasks, rather than practising each task alone (Detweiler & Lundy, 1995). There have been some striking examples of well practised participants being able to perform very complex tasks simultaneously. For example, Allport, Antonis, and Reynolds (1972) asked pianists to play music while shadowing speech. Shiffrin and Schneider's (1977) Theory of Automatic Processing relates to this issue. According to this theory, a novel task requires a great deal of effort and concentration to carry it out. This effort is called "controlled" processing. With practice, the task requires less effort and becomes automatic. Automatic tasks require less attentional capacity and are thus easier to combine with other tasks. This ability to automate tasks may decline with age, making it harder to combine tasks (Rogers, Bertus, & Gilbert, 1994). Even with practice, though, dual task interference effects do not necessarily disappear. Ruthruff, Johnston, and van Selst (2001) showed that when two tasks were combined such that the required responses were quite close together, practice did not eliminate interference. This effect is referred to as the refractory period, which basically means that when participants have to give responses to two different tasks in close succession there is a big drop-off in performance of the second response. This issue has been extensively investigated by researchers such as Pashler (1994a, 1994b), who suggests that this performance bottleneck reflects a structural limitation in the processing system (rather than being a result of, say, strategy of resource distribution, where participants choose to put most effort into the first task). Herath, Klingberg, Young, Amunts, and Roland (2001) investigated this issue using functional magnetic resonance imaging (fMRI—a brain imaging technique that allows researchers to plot which parts of the brain are active during performance of a particular task) and a visual task combined with a somatosensory task. Separately, each task used similar volumes of cortical and subcortical motor structures. When combined in such a way as to produce interference, an additional area—the right inferior frontal gyrus—seemed to be recruited to handle the interference. Similar arguments have been put forward by workers using the Evoked Response paradigm (evoked response techniques involve monitoring the electrical waves produced by the brain during a task). Nash and Fernandez (1996) and Luck (1998) both suggested that the P3 component of the event-related potential (ERP) showed interference from the second task in a refractory period experiment (see Chapter 2 for further details about ERPs).

To summarize, trying to divide our attention across several tasks involves a cost in terms of performance. The amount of this cost depends on how similar the tasks are, how demanding they are, and the degree to which they have been practised. Neurophysiological evidence to date has illustrated interference effects and suggests that additional brain areas, which are not involved in carrying out the tasks singly, may become involved in the dual task situation.

Control of attention

It is appropriate to consider the issue of attentional control immediately following the section on divided attention because it is now becoming clear that control processes play a major part in allowing us to carry out two tasks simultaneously. This issue was not discussed in any depth in the above section because traditional cognitive research has not really tackled the issue. This may in part be due to it requiring an individual differences type of methodology, e.g. looking at the extent to which individuals can dual task as a function of the efficiency of their control processes (it might help to note at this point that, in the neuropsychological literature, control processes are rapidly becoming synonymous with the frontal lobes, thus frontal lobe tasks could be used as an index of control processes). Neuropsychological research, however, has recently highlighted the role of control processes in the ability to dual task, illustrating how modern neuropsychological approaches can contribute new insights to cognitive psychology.

In our everyday lives, we do not have the impression of operating as if we were automatons, automatically responding to stimuli and events as they occur to us, like a Haitan zombie waiting for the next command from the voodoo priest. Instead, we use our judgement and predispositions to actively make decisions about what stimuli to attend to, and what strategies to adopt to achieve particular tasks. As you sit reading this book, think for a second about your motivation. Why are you reading this sentence right now? Will you still be reading this book in half an hour or will you have moved on to some other task or stimulation? Pause for a second and listen. What sounds can you hear? (as I sit here typing I am aware of tropical depression Iselle battering at my window). If you did pause and make a mental note of some stimulus going on in your environment, this demonstrates your free will, your ability to choose and to change the contents of your conscious awareness. (We will avoid the complex issue of whether free will can truly be said to exist at this point, but as a pause for thought consider this. Do not read the next sentence, but jump to the next paragraph. Hard isn't it, sometimes we just don't seem to have control over our actions!!)

The fact that participants can sit in psychology laboratories and take part in complex cognitive experiments by itself seems to indicate the existence of control processes. How else could participants listen to the sometimes convoluted instructions involved in such research and then attempt to carry them out, usually with a high degree of success. An influential paper by Allport and colleagues (Allport, Styles, & Hsieh, 1994) tried to down play the need to hypothesize the existence of specialist control processes. They asked participants to carry out a task, midway through which they had to switch to a different task. For example, the participants might be presented with a sequence of words that they had to read aloud in English. Following a cue they had to switch to reading in French. Allport et al. observed that even where the cue is given well in advance of the next stimulus, participants have real problems in changing from one set of task requirements to the other. This they suggest argues against the possibility of control processes, since a control process would enable a smooth switch from one task to the other. What these authors seem to neglect, however, is the fact that the participants do indeed manage to make the switch. They have listened to the instructions, encoded them, monitored the task, noted the presence of the cue, and changed to the second task. The switching process may involve costs but it also certainly involves control. If the participants failed to make the switch, then they would be exhibiting a pattern described by Duncan (1996) as "goal neglect". Duncan's views will be discussed in due course, as one attempt to explain the ways in which control processes can fail.

Clearly then, most of us would be inclined to the view that we have ongoing control of our cognitive processes; at any given moment we can decide what our priorities are and what we are going to attend to. This has led several major theorists to incorporate control mechanisms into their theoretical accounts of attention. For example, Baddeley, in his working memory model (Baddeley & Hitch, 1974) includes a component called the central executive (Figure 1.9). This controls the contents of the working memory buffer systems, namely the visuospatial scratchpad and the phonological loop.

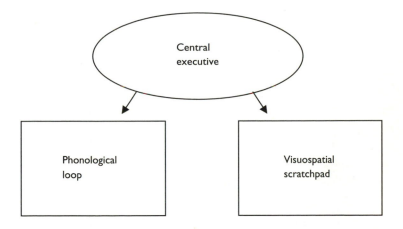

Figure 1.9 **The working memory model**
Information is retained in short-term memory using either a phonological process (the phonological loop) or visual imagery (the visuospatial scratchpad). Overseeing these subsystems is a control process called the central executive. Recently another component has been proposed, the episodic buffer.

Similarly, Shallice (1991) talks of the supervisory attentional system. This has been likened to Baddeley's notion of the central executive. It is a system for dealing with novelty, and over-riding the normal contingencies suggested by the environment. In recent years it has been realized that certain tasks make heavier demands on these control processes than other tasks. Such tasks can be characterized as requiring an ongoing high level of attention, e.g. they may require forward planning, monitoring of progress, or taking note of feedback. One such task is the Tower of Hanoi. In this task, participants have to solve a puzzle by obeying a series of simple rules. They are told that they must move three discs from the left peg to the right peg of a three peg board (Figure 1.10) by moving one disc at a time. At no time can a larger disc be placed upon a smaller disc. The task is to solve the puzzle as quickly as possible, using the smallest number of moves. The 3-disc problem requires 7 moves, the 4-disc problem 15.

Neuropsychological researchers soon noticed that difficulties on these tasks were associated with damage to a particular brain region, the frontal lobes (Shallice, 1982). Because of the widespread notion of "executive" functions, such deficits soon attracted the label "the dysexecutive syndrome" (e.g. Alderman & Ward, 1991). For many years this important area of cognitive functioning was neglected by

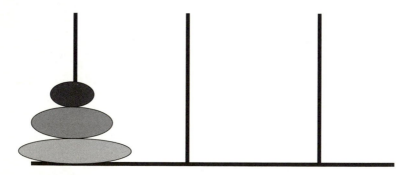

Figure 1.10   **The Tower of Hanoi**
The goal is to move the discs from the left to the right peg. One disc can be moved at a time, and a larger disc cannot be placed upon top of a smaller disc. The simplest version with three discs takes a minimum of seven moves.

researchers, but there has been an explosion of interest in the topic in the last 10 years. As we shall see in due course, much of this interest has been generated by the realization that patients could be enormously informative, and that "executive" deficits may be central to some very important and widespread disorders.

To summarize this section, control processes can be seen as vital to our understanding of attention. At any given moment we are making decisions about where best to concentrate our efforts and which stimuli to attend to. Certain tasks seem to involve these processes to a high degree, and certain patient groups with frontal lesions tend to be deficient on these tasks.

Vigilance

The final topic, which is often neglected in textbooks of cognitive psychology, is that of vigilance (or sustained attention). This topic has received some attention in the literature, but less than the other three topics we have mentioned.

The father of modern vigilance research is often cited as Mackworth (Mackworth, 1950). His area of interest is worth considering, since it is a good example of vigilance in everyday experience. During the Second World War, the Royal Air Force was conducting extensive bombing campaigns over enemy territory. The aircrew were subject to considerable stresses and strains once over the target area, but the flight to the target area was itself somewhat daunting. It would be conducted at altitude, and at a speed that by modern standards would be considered quite slow, so that it could be many hours after take-off by the time the objective was reached. Once in the air and on course the flight would be comparatively uneventful, and the flight crew's job quite monotonous. Add to this the cold, the time of night, and the relentless drone of the engines and you have a recipe for disaster. Not unlike modern long-distance lorry drivers, there was a real danger of pilot fatigue and, after a number of accidents, the War Office decided to investigate. Mackworth, then working at the Applied Psychology Unit in Cambridge (which was investigating a number of wartime issues), took on the task.

This was no easy problem to investigate. Bringing long-distance bomber conditions under experimental control was going to require some ingenuity. Mackworth's solution represented a considerable feat of engineering, illustrating the ingenious lengths some psychologists have been prepared to go to in order to bring their phenomenon into the laboratory. Mackworth constructed a replica of a bomber cockpit, complete with all the usual dials and instruments. These dials were linked by various cogs and wires such that they would simulate realistic flight values in a synchronized fashion. Built into this set-up was a clock, which the test pilots had to monitor very carefully. Very occasionally the second hand on the clock would behave in an unusual manner; it would tick over two seconds instead of one. The pilots had to monitor for this event and press a button whenever they noticed it occur. In this way, Mackworth was able to study pilots in a realistic cockpit environment, as they went through a simulated flight lasting many hours. He was then able to determine the performance decrements involved in such long and tedious tasks, as the pilots eventually fatigue and loose their ability to concentrate. Vigilance therefore refers to our ability to concentrate on a particular task over a period of time. It is important to all of us at some point in our lives, e.g. when undertaking a long-distance motorway journey. There are many occasions where being able to maintain vigilance becomes vital, e.g. in airline pilots. A related scenario is air traffic control, when a momentary lapse could prove disastrous and endanger hundreds of lives.

Detection of vigilance decrements in normal healthy participants usually requires a prolonged session with a monotonous task. For example, Botella, Contreras, Shih, and Rubio (2001) reported that short tests of sustained attention failed to find any decrements in two large samples of potential air traffic controllers. It has long been recognized that vigilance can be affected by pharmacological agents, and vigilance tasks have often been used in psychopharmacological trials. These tests are usually of the continuous performance type, in which the participant has to monitor a constantly changing succession of digits or letters, for a particular target. Such tests can be highly sensitive to reduced arousal, for example Graw et al. (2001) reported a performance decrement in the early morning following melatonin administration (alertness is usually good in the early morning).

Conversely, Amir et al. (2001) reported enhanced vigilance following caffeine administration. Finally, in monotonous tasks such as long-distance driving, certain behaviours may be a prelude to reduced vigilance and could therefore be used as an early warning. For example, drivers may begin to blink and open their eyes wide in an attempt to arouse themselves.

The ability to remain alert and responsive over a long period of time in the face of reduced stimulation (to maintain a vigil) is clearly an important skill. Most people are thankfully quite good at it, but can be impaired under certain circumstances. Typically this means after a very prolonged period, when fatigue starts to set in. Vigilance has not been widely studied in the laboratory, since it is difficult to persuade participants to take part in long and repetitive experiments. However, it is likely that this aspect of cognition will prove to be important when assessing patients, as we shall see in Chapter 7.

Summary

In this chapter we have seen how cognitive psychology has developed since the 1950s to explain the internal thought processes that take place in the human brain. We have seen how the topic of attention has been a central concern of much of this research. To date, psychologists have studied how we selectively attend to information, how we are able to divide our attention, the role of higher-order control processes, and finally how our attention declines over time as we become less vigilant. Chapter 2 will move on to describe the area of neuropsychology, and in particular the key assumptions and methods that underlie this approach.

Chapter 2

The role of
neuropsychology

Overview

THIS CHAPTER INTRODUCES the area of neuropsychology. It has been suggested that cognitive theories can help us to understand the problems experienced by clients with neurological disorders, and at the same time that observing client behaviour can lead us to modify those same cognitive theories. Thus modern cognitive neuropsychology represents a synergy between cognitive theory and clinical work. This chapter explains key assumptions underpinning neuropsychological research, e.g. the notion of a double dissociation. A number of widely used technological methods will also be explained. Coupled with the theory from Chapter 1, the reader should then be well set to appreciate the neuropsychological work on attention. The rest of the book will go on to show how these various theories and explanatory frameworks have been useful in the understanding of various neurological disorders and brain damage.

What is neuropsychology?

Neuropsychology is the application of psychological principles to the understanding and rehabilitation of brain damage. In recent years the principles being applied have been predominantly those originating from cognitive psychology. This application has been enormously successful, leading to the rapid development of neuropsychology as a leading specialty within clinical psychology (and it may become the first clinical specialty to branch out on its own—there are now divisions of neuropsychology in both the United Kingdom and the United States, with formal specialist training schemes in existence in the latter). At the same time, the ability of neuropsychological evidence to help resolve empirical issues has led to the approach becoming central to mainstream cognitive psychology.

Part of the reason why neuropsychology has been so successful in helping us to understand patients, and to advance cognitive theory, rests on a small number of fundamental assumptions held by workers in the field. We will now briefly consider these key assumptions, as they underlie much of the research work that will be presented in the later chapters.

Transparency

The first key assumption is transparency. It is assumed that when we assess a patient with a neurological condition, the patient previously had a normal cognitive system and the performance we observe is due to the brain damage they have suffered. For example, when Loken, Thornton, Otto, and Long (1995) tested the vigilance abilities of patients with head injury, it was assumed that prior to the head injury the patients would have been able to complete the vigilance task in a normal way. The deficit observed in comparison to the control group is therefore a result of the head injury.

The main threat to this assumption is that, following a neuro-logical insult, patients do not remain passive in the face of their difficulties. Instead, they will actively attempt to find strategies to cope with their problems. Also, there is the possibility of some recovery and reorganization of function following insult, which again will violate the assumption. Finally, there are some studies where the assumption of premorbid equivalence is suspect. Take, for example, the sometimes controversial topic of schizophrenia. This condition is increasingly being subject to a neuropsychological analysis. For example, Schneider (1976) looked at schizophrenic patients to see to what extent they were able to selectively attend to information in a dichotic listening task, compared to controls. There have been few studies attempting to look at preclinical schizophrenic patients, and it is far from clear that such patients ever had a "normal" cognitive system prior to developing the condition (this was partly the view put forward by the antipsychiatry movement, represented by psychiatrists such as Laing, i.e. that schizo-phrenics may have always been different, and should not be treated as ill simply because of that).

Modularity

The next key assumption is modularity. This suggests that the brain carries out a number of distinct cognitive operations, which are localized in different areas. Therefore, a patient can experience deficits in one system while other systems remain relatively spared and intact. Thus a patient with damage to the left temporal lobe may exhibit aphasia and have difficulty comprehending speech, but retain his or her ability to manipulate and remember visual images. Modularity is so fundamental to the modern cognitive enterprise that we need not go into specific examples, other than to say that this view fits in with much modern neuroscience, e.g. work showing the sophisticated specialization of the visual system (e.g. Hubel & Wiesel, 1979). A quick glance through any modern cognitive textbook will confirm the modular view as the predominant one in modern theories. For example, see Ellis and Young (1988) pages 31, 88, 116, 145, 181, 192, and 222 for modular accounts of object and face recognition, reading, and speech processing.

Neuropsychology has played a major role in supporting the modular view of cognitive processes. An early classic example of this comes from the domain of memory research. Theorists in the 1960s had suggested that memory can be conceived as operating through two separate systems, one for short-term memory the other for long-term memory. Short-term memory can be thought of as active, ongoing processing. An analogy is random access memory (RAM) on a computer. When information is to be manipulated it is loaded from the hard disc into RAM. Long-term memory is the storage of information over periods of time in which it has ceased to be actively processed; the computer analogy is the hard drive. In human terms, while you are reading this sentence it is being actively processed and you are retaining the words contained in the first part of the sentence in mind, so that you can use the context and meaning to understand the later parts and eventually comprehend the sentence as a whole and, clearly, as the sentence gets longer this becomes gradually more difficult, which is why we try and avoid writing unnecessarily long sentences such as this one. Once we stop actively processing information, we then have to rely on long-term memory, which is often remarkably poor at retaining material only briefly attended to. For example, it is unlikely now, even though you probably read it only a few minutes ago, that you can accurately recall the sentence which started off the previous paragraph. A longer-term example would be remembering what you had for breakfast yesterday.

Psychological theories popular in the late 1960s suggested that short-term and long-term memory were separate stores (Atkinson & Shiffrin, 1968), but it was difficult to definitively show this in clear-cut experimental studies. The alternative explanation—that memory consisted of a single store, with length of retention of material determined by the amount and type of processing it was subject to—could also account for most results (Craik & Lockhart, 1972). The key findings that pushed researchers towards favouring the former account came from neuropsychology, with publications such as that by Shallice and Warrington (1970). Shallice and Warrington (1970) showed that short-term memory processes could be dissociated from long-term memory. For example, a densely amnesic patient who can retain little or no new information over time, can nevertheless retain a given phone number over a short period of time, as long as he or she is not distracted and can go on attending to the task of keeping the numbers in mind (this procedure of asking people to repeat number sequences is commonly used to test short-term memory capacity, and most people can manage around seven numbers at a time). This kind of observation is known as a dissociation, i.e. short-term memory can dissociate from long-term memory, and it suggests that the two processes that dissociate may be separate, i.e. one can work without the other.

To give an analogy, if we were an alien species that had just landed on earth, and we were trying to figure out how a motor car works, we might carry out various tests and observations. Imagine that we come across a car in which the brake is malfunctioning, but we are still able to steer the car. We could conclude that the steering mechanism is independent of the brake. The two functions dissociate. Such a dissociation does not, however, prove the matter. It is always possible that the process that is impaired requires more brain capacity or resources to operate, leaving intact less difficult operations. In our analogy, the brake system may require more energy from the engine to

33

operate, and thus fails if the output from the engine is reduced while the steering remains intact. The solution to this dilemma is to find a second car, in which the steering is faulty while the brakes are intact. This second dissociation in the opposite direction rules out the suggestion that only the harder or more intensive process has been lost. Clearly, the fact that the brakes can work without the steering, and the steering can work without the brakes, suggests that these two systems are fully independent of each other.

Going back to the memory example, if short-term memory is intact in some patients who have severe long-term memory difficulties, this suggests that the processes are separate but it could also be the case that short-term memory simply requires less effort, resources, or capacity. What we need then, as in our analogy, is to find a patient with a dissociation in the opposite direction. Such patients have indeed been found, in other words people who can remember perfectly well what they were doing yesterday but struggle to retain even two numbers in mind for immediate recall. Their long-term memory is fine, their short-term memory is severely impaired. Such patients rule out the possibility that the original dissociation between an intact short-term memory and damaged long-term memory is simply due to the relative effort the two processes require.

To spell out this principle in clear terms, if there are two cognitive processes, A and B, and if a patient can do A but not B then this suggests that function A is independent of B. However, it may be that tasks testing function B are simply more difficult and are impaired by general brain damage, which typically impairs total brain capacity (e.g. speed of processing is much slower, as we shall see in Chapter 4). This possibility can be ruled out if we can find a second patient with the opposite dissociation, who can't do A but can do B. This pattern of two patients, one who can do A and not B, and another who can't do A but can do B is called a double dissociation. It was such patterns of impairment in patients that eventually led to cognitive psychologists generally accepting the view that memory consists of at least two separate processes, short term and long term.

Researchers quickly realized that this was a powerful technique, and since cognitive theories are generally modular in nature it rapidly came to be applied in many different domains, with researchers seeking to validate the view that one process was separate and distinct from another. An example from the domain we are primarily focused upon in this book, that of attention, was published by Gregory et al. (2002). These workers examined patients with dementia, in particular Alzheimer's disease. Alzheimer's disease accounts for the majority of elderly patients with dementia, and consists of a distinctive pathology within the brain. The plaques and tangles that are present are thought to be formed during the pathological process of neuronal death and loss as the brain atrophies. Recently, researchers have sought to differentiate patients where the pathology is localized within a particular area of the brain, and one such subcategory is frontal variant frontotemporal dementia. In these patients the pathology (i.e. neuronal loss) is thought to be concentrated in the frontal areas of the brain, and thus their condition may help us to understand the brain processes served by these regions. Thus Gregory et al. (2002) compared Alzheimer's patients with a typical pattern of deficits with those thought to have predominantly frontal pathology. The study set out to find evidence that frontal parts of the brain are responsible for processing higher-order concepts in problems requiring an understanding of human agency. Such problems are sometimes said to involve "theory of mind". For example, consider this story.

> Simon and James are sitting in the library one day when James says to Simon that he is going up to the second floor to see if he can find a book he needs. On the way up the stairs he meets Jane, who stops to chat and suggests that they go for lunch together. So James and Jane go down the stairs and leave the library to have lunch together in the café across the road. While they are having lunch Jane asks James if he has seen Simon, and James replies "Yes", and explains that he was working in the library on the first floor. Meanwhile, back in the library, Simon has gone to look for James.

At this point we can ask a number of questions. If Jane decides to go and look for Simon, where will she go? And where will Simon be heading to try and find James? Problems such as this require us to keep quite a bit of information in mind, and to code that information in a very particular way. As the scenario progresses, we can distinguish between the current state of affairs and the state of affairs as they exist in the minds of the characters involved. So at the end of the scenario, James and Jane are in the café and Simon is somewhere looking for James. Simon believes that James is on the second floor, while Jane and James think that Simon is on the first floor. To answer the questions posed we have to refer to the state of mind of the characters, and not to the actual state of affairs as they have developed. Thus we should say that Jane will head to the first floor to find Simon and Simon will go to the second floor to find James. If we had not been keeping careful track of these developments, and in particular to the beliefs of the individuals, then we might say that Simon will look for James in the café, since we know that that is where James actually is, forgetting that Simon does not know this since that development occurred after James met Jane on the stairs. Certain kinds of patient groups have been found to have difficulties with these types of problem, particularly patients with autism. It would be interesting, therefore, if we could establish that this function is served by the frontal lobes, as Gregory et al.'s study sets out to do. What they found was that frontal variant patients had difficulty with the theory of mind problems, but their memory remained relatively intact. Conventional Alzheimer's patients, however, were able to solve the theory of mind problems (except the more complicated ones involving second-order attributions) but were impaired in their memory performance. This interesting study therefore suggests that patients with predominantly frontal pathology are specifically impaired on theory of mind problems, but not on memory tasks, while other patients without the focused frontal pathology have impaired memory but their theory of mind performance remains intact. That these two abilities should dissociate is interesting, because it suggests that the frontal variant patients genuinely have a theory of mind deficit, i.e. an inability to attribute to another a particular view that differs from their own perspective. An alternative account might suggest that the theory of mind difficulty in these patients is due to a memory failure. In other words, the theory of mind scenarios are quite complex and require quite a lot of detailed information to be kept in mind. In failing to maintain this information, what is lost is the individual beliefs, not the current state of the scenario. Such an alternative account is ruled out by the

THE ROLE OF NEUROPSYCHOLOGY

observation that the Alzheimer's patients can solve the theory of mind scenarios despite having considerable memory difficulties.

Thus we have seen how double dissociations can provide important confirmatory evidence about assertions being made in cognitive theory. As will be seen, this has been the rationale behind a considerable amount of research in the field. However, we should not make the mistake of assuming it is the only rationale. Many studies with patients set out simply to describe the types of deficit associated with particular conditions. Often this is intended to help improve decision making such as diagnosis, treatment, and rehabilitation. Such studies can be very useful in helping us to localize function to particular brain areas and structures. Some studies set out to determine to what extent a function can be rehabilitated or will spontaneously improve, and again this can greatly aid our understanding of cognitive functions.

Connectionism

Having just discussed the issue of modularity it might be useful at this point to discuss a possible point of confusion or perplexity that students might have about this assumption and other types of theory currently prevalent within neuroscience and cognitive psychology. Those who have studied cognitive psychology will be aware that there is a class of theory that does not follow the assumption of modularity, and that appears quite different to traditional cognitive theories. These are the theories that arise from connectionism, sometimes referred to as neural networks. Connectionism is a recent trend within cognitive psychology in which models are built from simple neuron-like units connected together in layers. Because they are made up of these simpler constituents, such models are often referred to as neural networks (Figure 2.1). In such models, information passes between successive layers of interconnected units. They have the attraction of biological plausibility, since the brain is itself made up of neurons, although in reality the neural network components are many thousands of times simpler than a typical neuron in the human central nervous system (even on the basis of our currently very limited understanding of such neurons).

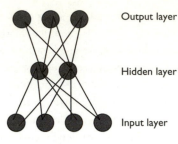

Output layer

Hidden layer

Input layer

Figure 2.1 **A simple neural network**
These networks typically consist of three layers of simple neuron-like units. Patterns are presented to the input units and fed through the network to produce an output at the output layer.

A further attraction of these kinds of theory is that the networks appear to organize themselves according to the application of learning algorithms. Consider a simple example. Imagine that we want to build a very simple network that can classify a small set of objects as either living or man made. We could have each input node represent a particular item. So if we want to present the object "cat" to the network, we activate the "cat" node. Activation from this node passes through the hidden layer and then on to the output layer, where we want the "living" node to activate. Input patterns such as "cat" are presented to the network many times and activations allowed to pass through. The network is reinforced to give the required response "living" through the application of the learning algorithm. Eventually, a point will be reached where the response "living" will be activated when we present the object "cat" and likewise for "dog", whereas "table" and "chair" will cause "non-living" to activate. Note that this is a very simplistic example, and not at all serious. For example, a serious attempt at a model of living versus non-living categorization would probably have features and functions as the inputs.

Having made such a model, we can now see how it functions in other contexts. Such networks are for example able to make accurate generalizations and predictions. We might also "lesion" the model, e.g. by removing some nodes or connections and then seeing how it performs. It would be interesting if the damaged network happens to behave like particular patients with deficits in that domain.

We will discuss this approach and its merits in a later chapter. For the time being, suffice it to say that such models can appear to be very different to traditional cognitive theories. In particular, they do not look modular in nature, and they are often said to use "parallel" processing, in other words a number of features are input to the network and they all progress through the network simultaneously to produce an output. For example, a network representing word reading might have inputs for individual letters, word shape, and context, all of which simultaneously progress through the network to produce the output (which might be conceptualized as activation of semantics, or perhaps an output such as speaking the word).

As will be argued later, the connectionist approach is not really incompatible with traditional cognitive theories. Instead, we can conceive neural networks as helping us to think through what happens inside the traditional boxes of cognitive theories. Work in the field of connectionism has now reached the point where researchers have realized that accomplishing complex real-world tasks is going to require large-scale modular neural networks, which rapidly start to resemble the traditional box and arrow diagrams (Figure 2.2). In other words, if we are trying to get a computer to recognize objects and speak their name, we might have a network that takes the input from a video camera and digitizes it, another network that examines the image to try and pick out features, a network that examines the features to identify objects, a network that takes the object label and outputs the appropriate phonology, and a final network that drives the speech synthesizer.

Imaging techniques

Finally in this chapter, which serves as a basis for the theoretical ones that follow, it will be useful to briefly outline modern imaging techniques. Many studies in the literature employ a variety of sophisticated technological research methods, designed to reveal knowledge of brain structures and localization of function. This will be clearly seen in Chapter 5, when the localization of selective attention processes is discussed. The main techniques to be considered are the

ATTENTION

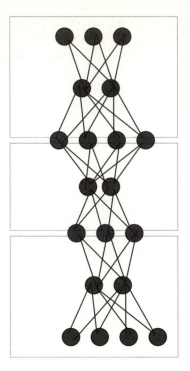

Figure 2.2 **A complex neural network**
This complex neural network consists of three simpler networks connected together. Information is passed from one network to another. Such models can be seen as similar to traditional modular box and arrow style theories used in cognitive neuropsychology.

electroencephalogram (EEG) and the related event-related potential (ERP) method, positron emitted tomography (PET), and nuclear magnetic resonance imaging (NMRI).

Electroencephalography and ERPs

The activity of the neurons in the brain results in chemical electrical discharge, which varies depending on the level of brain activity. This results in a constantly fluctuating small electrical potential on the scalp, which can be detected by electrodes, usually with reference to another part of the body away from the scalp (i.e. the EEG is the difference between the potential on the scalp and that measured at, say, the ankle).

When a stimulus is presented to a participant a wave of processing progresses through the brain, which results in a systematic change in the EEG. This wave is known as the evoked response potential (ERP), and can be evoked by either visual (vERP) or auditory (aERP) stimuli. The evoked response potential is fairly uniform, and parts of the wave have been labelled by researchers (Figure 2.3), so that negative peaks are labelled N1, N2, etc., and positive peaks are labelled P1, P2, etc., with P3 representing a large positive peak that typically occurs about 300 ms after stimulus presentation (and is therefore often labelled the P300). By presenting many stimuli and averaging the wave over many trials, a representation of what the ERP looks like in various experimental manipulations can be built up, e.g. varying stimulus intensity, required response, etc.

Considerable research has gone into examining aspects of the ERP under various conditions. For example, one of the early findings is that the amplitude of the P300 is often enlarged if a stimulus is

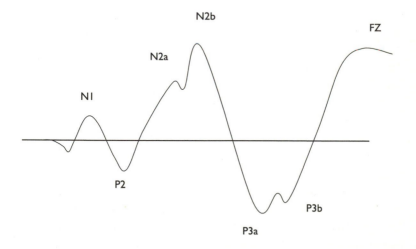

Figure 2.3 **The components of an evoked response potential (ERP), showing some of the N and P components.**

unexpected. The ERP technique is undoubtedly useful as an index to various processes and an indicator of different stages of processing. The time resolution is very fine grained, with analysis being possible over a course of milliseconds following stimulus presentation. This fine-grained temporal resolution sits well with many cognitive experiments. However, the technique reveals little about how structure relates to function, and for this reason many researchers have turned to PET and MRI techniques.

Positron emission tomography (PET)

Positron emission tomography is a technique that allows researchers to find out which parts of the brain are most active. Participants are injected with a radioactive tracer, such as water in which the oxygen atom has been made unstable so that it eventually will emit a single positron. This then circulates in the body and can be detected with special apparatus. Greater concentrations of the substance indicate regions of greater blood flow, and in the brain these are thought to reflect areas of increased metabolic activity. Thus a PET scan of the brain indicates which areas are most active.

If a PET scan is combined with a subtraction methodology, it is possible to use the technique to look at quite fine aspects of cognition. For example, imagine if we wanted to find out which part of the brain is involved in vigilance, i.e. keeping alert over a long period of time in order to detect an infrequent stimulus. We might ask our participant to observe a screen on which a constantly changing sequence of numbers is being presented. Presumably the PET scan would then indicate which parts of the brain are responsible for the basic processes involved in perceiving the changing stream of numbers. If we then ask the person to look out for a particular number, the PET scan should reveal not only which parts of the brain are perceiving the numbers but which additional areas are involved in maintaining the vigil. If we subtract the first scan from the second, i.e. remove the activation due to basic perceptual processes, what we should be left with is the activation due to maintaining the vigil (Figure 2.4).

PET scanning has been widely used because of its ability to reveal which areas of the brain are involved in particular functions.

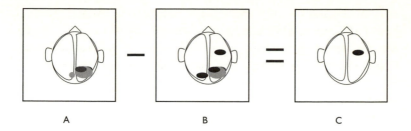

Figure 2.4 **Methodology for functional PET scanning**
In each diagram the shaded areas represent regions of greatest cerebral blood flow, with darker areas representing greatest flow. In A, the participant is observing a constantly changing stimuli, whereas in B he/she is observing and looking out for a particular target. When the two are subtracted, as in C, the remaining activation is presumed to be that which is specific to looking out for a particular target. (Note that this is a hypothetical example.)

However, the temporal and spatial resolution is poor. Thus we cannot examine the execution of tasks with millisecond resolution or pin-point precise anatomical areas involved in particular functions.

Nuclear magnetic resonance imaging (NMRI)

NMRI is based upon the physics of magnetism. The person to be scanned is placed in close proximity to a powerful magnetic field and a radio frequency pulse is then emitted. This pulse causes a resonance in the atomic nuclei, which can be detected by sensors placed around the body, allowing a detailed and high-resolution image to be constructed of the tissues. The technique can also be combined with an analysis of oxygenated versus non-oxygenated blood contrast, allowing a picture to be built up of which brain tissues are most active, as with PET (it is then referred to as fNMRI). Thus accurate images, with 2-mm resolution, can be constructed, coupled with information about brain activity. The technique is rapidly being adopted and has been used in a great many studies. Generally, a similar subtraction methodology is used to that illustrated for PET scan studies, where tasks with different cognitive demands are contrasted. Both PET and NMRI are undoubtedly impressive and extremely useful techniques that have been widely used and no doubt will be of increasing interest in the future. However, both techniques are limited in terms of the possible time resolution when looking at brain functions, and this may limit their usefulness when looking at some of the very fine-grained aspects of cognition.

Summary

This chapter has described how neuropsychology has come to be an important part of the discipline of cognitive psychology. The performance of brain-damaged patients is assumed to reflect damage to cognitive processes in a fairly transparent way. Cognitive theories can therefore help us to understand such brain damage.

Traditional cognitive theories have been modular in nature and support for such a modular organization of the brain has come from neuropsychology, primarily through the elaboration of double dissociations. Indeed, the connectionist or neural network approach can sometimes seem to be somewhat at odds with traditional cognitive theories. However, as such models evolve to become modular in nature there will be increased synergy between the types of theory. Network models will help us to elaborate the microscopic functions, while traditional theories explain the macroscopic relationships between different functions. The various technological scanning methods that are used to discover brain structure and function are also expected to become more useful as they gain in sophistication.

To this point we have covered the various cognitive theories of attention, and looked at the nature and fundamental assumptions of neuropsychology. We are now almost ready to go on and consider the research literature relating theories of attention to patients with neurological conditions. However, before doing so it will be helpful if we are also familiar with some of the principal psychological tests that have been used to examine attention in patients. They constantly recur in different research studies, and thus it will save much repetition if we are acquainted with them at the outset. This is the aim of Chapter 3.

Chapter 3

Assessment of attention

Overview

THIS CHAPTER DESCRIBES and illustrates a number of the more important tests that have been used by clinical psychologists to evaluate the attention skills of patients. These tests have been widely used in research. It is essential, therefore, that, before going on to consider work done on specific conditions, the reader is familiarized with the various measures used.

The backbone of neuropsychological assessment in the United Kingdom and to some degree the United States, has been the Weschler Adult Intelligence Scale (WAIS). Consequently we start with a review of the WAIS, and then move on to other traditional tests. The chapter then describes developments over the last decade, which has seen the rise of specialist batteries devoted to attention. Finally, there is speculation as to possible future directions in the assessment of this important function.

Use of the Weschler Adult Intelligence Scale

Traditionally, the assessment of attention by neuropsychologists has relied on the Weschler Adult Intelligence Scale (WAIS). This can be supplemented by a variety of additional tests such as verbal fluency and the Wisconsin Card Sorting task (WCST) (Parker & Crawford, 1992).

The WAIS has been around since the middle of the twentieth century (Weschler, 1955) and remains one of the most widely used measures in clinical psychology practice. Virtually all trainee clinical psychologists will receive extensive training in its administration and interpretation.

The WAIS was not originally designed as a neuropsychological assessment instrument. Rather, it was intended to provide a reliable estimate of overall ability, based on a broad range of very different tests. These were put together by Weschler, based on the kinds of tests in use at that time (the late 1930s). Individual subtests of the WAIS can often trace their lineage back to much earlier tests, e.g. those used for selection purposes by the US army in the First World War. However,

Weschler's original selection proved to be well chosen, tapping a range of different mental abilities. Thus, as neuropsychologists began looking around for useful instruments, they were pleased to find that the WAIS gave a good all-round picture of performance. It turned out to be sensitive to lesions in a variety of brain areas.

In the domain of attention, two subtests from the battery have been viewed as good measures of this aspect of functioning. The Block Design task requires the testee to construct designs from blocks that have alternately coloured faces (Figure 3.1). This requires a fair degree of planning and strategizing, especially for the harder items. It is generally thought to be sensitive to frontal lobe lesions (Lezak, 1983).

The other subtest is the Digit Symbol task, in which the testee is confronted by a number grid, with numbers 1 to 9 alongside a variety of symbols. Below this is a longer sequence of numbered boxes (Figure 3.2). The task is to copy the appropriate symbol from the grid above into the box alongside the number in the lower grid. The testee is given 2 minutes to copy as many symbols as possible. This test is thought to reflect the ability to sustain concentration over the period of the task. Like all WAIS subtests, poor performance could be attributed to a number of factors. Because of this, interpretation requires experience and the bringing together of several sources of information. For example, the Digit Symbol subtask also depends on good manual dexterity. Memory may also be involved (since as the test progresses some testees will learn which symbols are associated with which numbers). Performance on other tasks can rule out such possibilities, allowing the clinician to narrow down the likely source of any impairment. More recent versions of the test have also included additional subtests to help in interpreting performance. Thus there is now a copy task, which is a purer measure of perception and dexterity.

Experienced clinicians do not rely solely on WAIS performance to come to a judgement about a client's attentional capacities; a detailed case history is also necessary, and inferences based on observing the client's performance and demeanour across the whole range of testing will also be made. Thus it would be noted if a client appeared unusually fatigued at the end of a testing session, compared

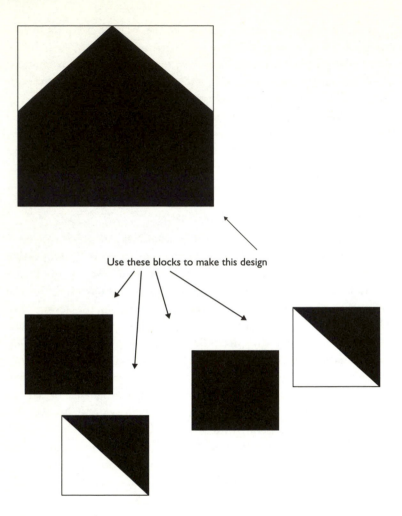

Figure 3.1 **Block design task**
A number of coloured blocks (like the four shown here) have to be put together to make a complex pattern, such as that at the top. In the actual test, up to nine blocks are required for some of the harder patterns.

to the start (van Zomeren & Brouwer, 1992). In addition, most clinicians seek to supplement the information gained from the WAIS with additional tests from outside the battery.

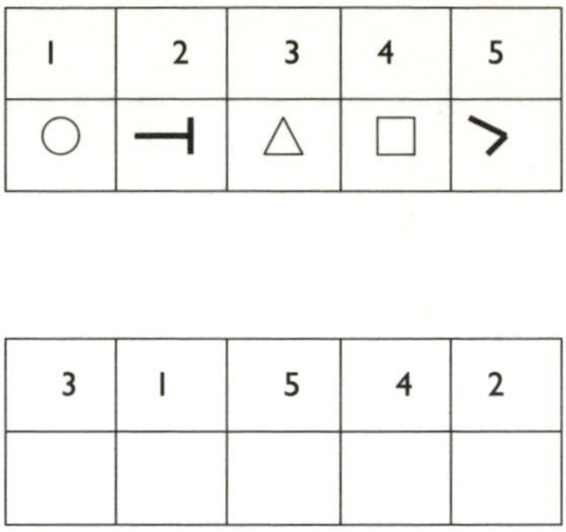

1	2	3	4	5
○	⊢	△	☐	＞

3	1	5	4	2

Figure 3.2 **A digit symbol task, similar to that in the WAIS**
The participant has to copy, as quickly as possible, the shapes from the upper grid that correspond to the randomly ordered sequence in the lower grid. So the first square needs a triangle, then a circle, etc.

Other traditional tests used in the assessment of attention

The domain that is most frequently expanded on is frontal lobe functioning. Thus the Tower of Hanoi and its derivatives, such as the Tower of London (Shallice, 1982), require the testee to plan a sequence of moves in an unfamiliar task to achieve a goal. In the case of the Tower of Hanoi (see Figure 1.10), the goal is to move all the discs from the left-most to the right-most peg by moving only one disc at a time and at no time placing a larger disc onto a smaller one.

Fluency tasks involve asking patients to generate as many words as they can beginning with a particular letter, typically F, A, and S, or belonging to a particular category, e.g. animals (Benton, 1986). Normal participants typically use strategies to facilitate performance, e.g. recalling from categories, whereas frontal patients recall single words at random, often with a high degree of repetition.

In the Wisconsin Card Sorting task (WCST; Milner, 1963), the patient is presented with four stimulus cards, which differ from each other in a variety of ways. In fact, they have different numbers of different shapes in different colours (Figure 3.3). The testee is given a deck of cards that they have to try and sort according to the three rules available (they are not initially made aware of the rules). To do

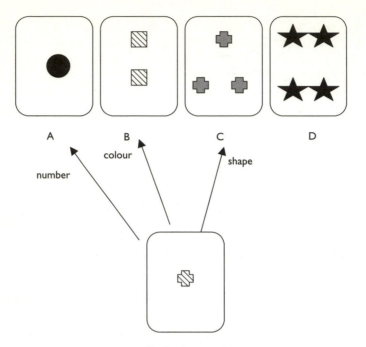

A   B   C   D

colour

number

shape

Card to be sorted

Figure 3.3 **The Wisconsin Card Sorting task (WCST)**
Four target cards are laid before the participant, who has to try and work
out the rule the examiner is thinking of by sorting each card. In this case,
the card could be sorted according to number (a), colour (b), or shape (c).
Note that in the version that is most widely used by clinicians, the cards to be
sorted will only match one rule at a time (thus in this example there would
not be any cards showing three crosses, as this would match card C on
both rules, making it hard for the examiner to judge which one the client
intended).

this the testee is instructed to place a card underneath one of the
stimulus cards; if it matches a rule the examiner is thinking of then the
examiner will say "correct", if it does not match a rule the examiner
will say "incorrect". In fact, the testee determines the first rule to be
used, since the examiner will say correct to the first legitimate rule that
is chosen. After a certain number of correct matches, the rule is
changed without telling the testee, who has to realize that a change

has occurred and work out what the next rule is. Nowadays, most clinicians use Nelson's (1978) modification of the task, which is both simpler to score and easier to administer than the original. It is also less stressful to the testees, as they are told when the rule has changed. Frontal patients typically find it very difficult to move beyond the first rule they discover and will commit many perseverative responses, i.e. continue to follow the now invalid rule despite receiving feedback that it has changed.

The Trails Task (Reitan, 1958) looks at people's ability to alternate rapidly between response sets. Thus testees initially complete a sort of dot-to-dot task, joining up numbered circles. This is immediately followed by a version in which they again have to join up dots, but this time alternating between numbers and letters of the alphabet, e.g. 1–A–2–B–3–C, etc. (Figure 3.4) The latter is much harder and typically takes quite a few seconds longer. Frontal patients often find the task very difficult, having to be reminded to alternate

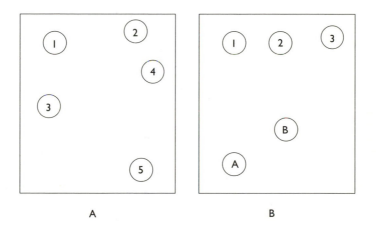

A   B

Figure 3.4 **Trail making tasks**
The participant first of all has to simply connect together, as fast as possible, a sequence of numbered circles, as shown in A. This is an index of drawing speed. In part B, the participant has to alternate between numbers and letters, i.e. connecting 1 to A to 2 to B to 3, etc. Participants are invariably slower at the latter, showing the cost that accrues from having to switch mental sets between numbers and letters.

many times, and frequently failing to complete the task in less than 5 minutes.

A similar task is the Stroop task. Like the Trails test, this is usually administered in two parts. In the first part, the testee simply names the colours of a list of coloured Xs as fast as possible. In the second part the testee has to identify the colours of incongruent words, e.g. the word "red", written in green ink. In the latter task, the word itself causes considerable interference in naming the colour, since words are easily read and their meaning instantly available. As with the Trails test, patients with frontal lobe lesions typically find this very hard, frequently reading out the words and having to be reminded to say the colour. Unlike normal participants, they are unable to inhibit the rapid and highly automated normal reading response that occurs to a word stimulus.

A number of clinicians use the Rey–Osterrieth Complex Figure task as an indicator of frontal dysfunction. In this task, patients have to copy a complex abstract figure, made up of a number of components (Figure 3.5). A short while later (typically after a 3-minute delay) they have to try and draw the figure from memory. Frontal patients tend to make a very poor and disorganized copy, and subsequently are able to recall very little of the figure from memory (Osterrieth, 1944).

Other domains of functioning within attention have traditionally been assessed much less frequently. As van Zomeren and Brouwer (1992) point out, simple and choice reaction times could be administered to assess basic speed of processing, but rarely are. Instead, the Paced Auditory Serial Additions Task (PASAT), Gronwall (1977) has been widely used. In this task, the patient hears a list of numbers being read out on a tape at a set speed, e.g. one number every 2 seconds. The task is to shout out the sum of each successive pair of numbers, without any omissions (Figure 3.6). The task is quite complex, involving a number of aspects of working memory. To complete the task it is necessary to remember the last number, listen for the next, add the two together, shout out the sum, remember what the last number was, listen for the next, and so on.

As Gronwall and Wrightson (1974) pointed out, patients often have problems at particular speeds, and presenting the numbers at

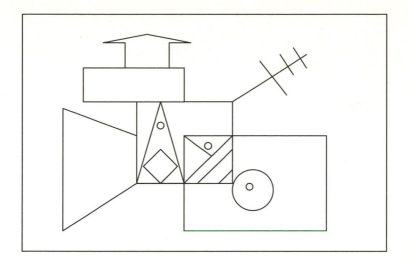

Figure 3.5 **The Rey–Osterrieth Complex Figure task**
The participant is shown a complex, abstract line drawing such as that shown above and asked to copy it. The copy is then scored for accuracy. After a delay, the participant is asked to draw the complex figure. The difference between the two scores represents what they have retained.

different rates allows the examiner to determine the optimum speed for each patient. There have, however, been a number of criticisms of this test. Bruins and Nieuwenhuizen (1990) found that performance was correlated with speed of making additions, while Ward (1997) found that in some circumstances young normal participants could perform worse than older subjects matched for age (perhaps the result of less emphasis being put on learning number bonds in modern education). Van Zomeren and Brouwer (1992) point out alternative simple strategies for assessing speed of processing, e.g. taking the initial control portion of either the Trails or Stroop tasks as indications of simple speed.

Other than observing patients during the course of testing, sustained attention and vigilance have infrequently been assessed in routine clinical practice. This is probably because of the lack of a good, widely available, standardized instrument for the adult population. Where it has been assessed, this has usually been via some type of

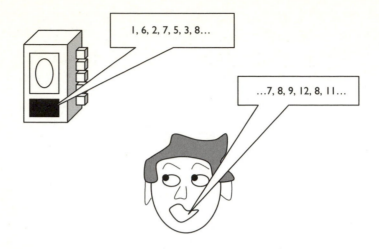

Figure 3.6 **The Paced Auditory Serial Additions task (PASAT)**
A series of spoken numbers is played to the participant, at a set rate (often
one number per 2 seconds in clinical settings). The participant has to listen
to the first two numbers and then shout out the sum, in this case 1 + 6 = 7.
The participant then has to listen to each subsequent number and shout out
the sum of this plus the immediately preceding number, in other words
summing all possible pairs. In this case this is 6 + 2 = 8, then 2 + 7 = 9, etc.

continuous performance test such as that developed by Rosvold,
Mirsky, Sarason, Bransome, and Beck (1956). As mentioned in
Chapter 7, such tests have been widely used with children in whom
attention deficit disorder is suspected. As described below in relation
to the Test of Everyday Attention, vigilance measures have in recent
years become available for adult assessment. As a result, the clinical
picture may well now have changed, with this aspect being much more
routinely assessed.

To summarize this chapter to this point, we have seen that
clinical assessment to date has been largely based upon the use of
the WAIS. Two subtests of the WAIS in particular have been thought
to assess attention: the Digit Symbol task and the Block Design
task. The former has been thought to reflect concentration and
the latter frontal lobe functioning. This basic approach has then been
supplemented by the use of a variety of additional tasks, most of

which are thought to expand upon the domain of frontal lobe functioning, with some tests reflecting speed of processing. In adults, vigilance and sustained attention have often not been assessed other than via clinical observation of the testing session (which will frequently last several hours).

Recent developments — specialized batteries for attention

Developments in neuropsychology during the 1990s began to change this pattern. Specific tests and batteries are being developed to assess particular functional domains, and these are often based on the latest theoretical thinking within the discipline (whereas the WAIS was originally put together based upon clinical intuition and common sense, reflecting views on general intelligence current at that time). As clinicians become more confident in the new instruments that are being developed, there may be a move away from the use of general batteries such as the WAIS towards specialist instruments in particular domains. This could well be facilitated by the use of quicker, general screening instruments that can point the way towards which areas need to be assessed in more depth (see, for example, Ward, 2002).

In recent years a number of specialist tests have been developed for the assessment of attention, for example the Test of Everyday Attention (TEA; Robertson, Ward, Ridgeway, & Nimmo-Smith [1994] note that the current author has an interest in the following discussion as a co-author of this test). Following the rationale behind the Rivermead Behavioural Memory test (Wilson, Cockburn, & Baddeley, 1985), the TEA sets out to be an ecologically valid assessment of attention. In other words, as far as possible the tests were designed to reflect realistic tasks that people might have to carry out in everyday life. The intention is to give a better prediction of functional capacities than has sometimes been observed with more abstract laboratory-style tasks. Further, the authors set out to devise a set of tests that reflects current theoretical views on attention. Thus measures were devised of selective attention, flexibility (i.e. switching), divided attention, and sustained attention. In several cases both auditory and visual measures were provided. Subsequent factor analysis of the normative data suggested that the battery was successful in tapping these various aspects of attention, and that the measures were valid alongside other traditional measures, e.g. the Paced Auditory Serial Additions task (PASAT) and Wisconsin Card Sorting task (WCST; see above). Novel features of the battery that have come to be much appreciated by clinicians include the provision of a well-standardized dual task measure and a vigilance test.

To give readers a flavour of the kinds of tests included in the TEA, some of the more important ones will be briefly described. As a measure of visual selective attention, patients have to search a large map containing lots of symbols, circling one symbol in particular. Auditory versions using tone discrimination are also included. A further visual search task requires patients to look through pages from a telephone directory, looking for particular symbols. When combined with a tone counting task, this gives a good measure of divided attention ability. In the author's experience, this is a good measure of frontal lobe functioning (as would be expected from recent research; see Chapter 6). Frontal patients are often completely unable to dual task, often having to stop searching completely while they count the tones. They then try and search quickly in the short gaps between tone sequences. The overall result is a large dual task decrement score (dual tasking ability is measured via a single index that incorporates both aspects of performance, i.e. number of symbols found and number of tones counted correctly). A further frontal measure is attention switching. In this task patients have to count sequences of lift (i.e. elevator) doors, as if they were going up and down in a lift. Just as in real life, lifts can move up and down, thus on appropriate signals the patients have to reverse their direction of counting, finally indicating which floor they think the lift ends up at. The test showed a significant correlation with performance on the WCST, and frontal lobe patients are frequently unable to reverse direction of counting when they encounter the cues to switch (Figure 3.7). Finally, sustained attention is assessed on a long and repetitive task in which patients have to listen to a long list of numbers for a particular target (they are told that they are listening for lottery ticket numbers). The task lasts for 10 minutes and there are 10 targets. Again, in the current author's clinical experience, this task is sensitive to vigilance

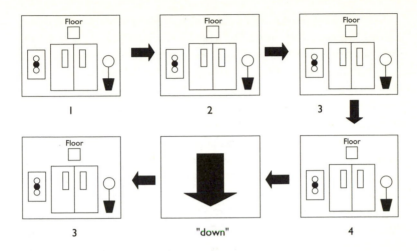

Figure 3.7 Illustration of the lift task from the Test of Everyday Attention (TEA)

The participant has to count each lift picture, as if the lift were ascending or descending. In doing this he or she follows the path indicated by the small arrows between boxes. Every so often, a box with a large arrow inside, pointing either up or down, is encountered. This indicates that the lift has made a stop, and will move off afterwards in the direction indicated, either up or down. The participant then has to continue counting, either up or down, as indicated. Finally, he or she arrives at the final lift and give the final floor. In this example, required responses are indicated under each box. So the participant would count "1, 2, 3, 4, down, 3". The arrows thus indicate changes in the direction of counting, which is problematic for many patients with frontal lesions.

deficits, which can be very striking in stroke patients with unilateral left neglect (see Chapter 5)

Following on from the success of the TEA, Manly, Robertson, Anderson, and Nimmo-Smith (1998); Manly, Anderson, Nimmo-Smith, Turner, Watson, and Robertson (2001) went on to develop a similar battery for children (called the Test of Everyday Attention for Children—TEACh). This has become a highly influential battery amongst clinicians working with children and, as will be seen in Chapter 6, the measure of sustained attention it contains has been found to be specifically impaired in children with attention deficit hyperactivity disorder.

In terms of frontal lobe functioning, Wilson, Alderman, Burgess, Emslie, Evans (1996) published the Behavioural Assessment of the Dysexecutive Syndrome (BADS). This contains a number of realistic tasks, validated against traditional measures and shown to be sensitive to frontal lobe lesions. Clinicians will be particularly interested to know that it contains a version of the Six Elements task. As will be discussed in Chapter 6, this has been put forward in several clinical studies as one of the best measures of frontal lobe functioning, showing increased sensitivity over a number of traditional measures such as the WCST. In the Six Elements task, the testees are given a number of subtasks to carry out in a 10-minute period (Figure 3.8). The tasks are such that all the subtasks cannot be completed within the 10 minutes. The testees are told that they will earn maximum credit for carrying out at least some of each of the various subtasks. Thus the ideal strategy is one in which the testee carries out a bit of each subtask and then moves on, to ensure that at least some of each is completed in the time allowed. This requires some planning and monitoring during task execution. Typically, frontal patients have difficulty following the instructions and work their way through the subtasks, completing each in turn. By the end of the time allowed only a fraction of the required subtasks have been attempted, resulting in a low score.

The last battery to be described is designed to assess particular difficulties that are frequently experienced by patients following stroke. This involves the phenomenon of neglect (often referred to as unilateral neglect), in which a patient fails to attend to the environment on the side of the body contralateral to the lesion site. So patients who experience a stroke affecting the right side of their brain will frequently fail to pay attention to the left side of their environment. This is most noticeable in the visual domain, where patients may fail to see the left side of objects, or not read words on the left side of a page. A specialized battery of tests has been put together to identify unilateral neglect, again using realistic tasks resembling real-world activities. This is the Behavioural Inattention Test (BIT; Wilson, Cockburn, & Halligan, 1987). For example, one task involves placing before the patient a life-sized photograph of a breakfast tray, and asking the patient to describe what he or she has been given for breakfast (Figure 3.9). Stroke patients with one-sided neglect will

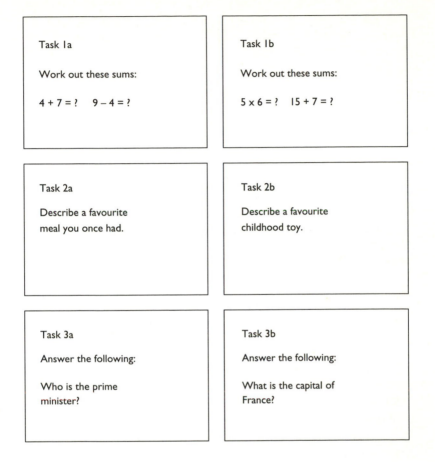

Figure 3.8 **The Six Elements task**
The participant is presented with six subtasks. There are three types of task, each of which has a part a and b. The participants are told to complete as many of the tasks as possible in 10 minutes, and that they will get most credit for the earlier items in each subtask. They are also told that for each of the main three task types they are not allowed to go straight from version a to b. An optimal strategy therefore would involve doing approximately 1 minute and 40 seconds of each subtask in the order 1a, 2a, 3a, 1b, 2b, 3b. This, however, requires considerable co-ordination and task monitoring, something that patients with frontal lesions find difficult.

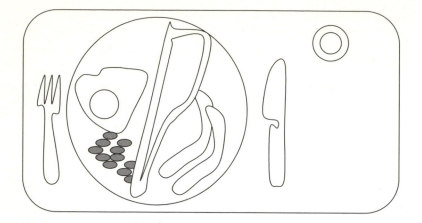

Figure 3.9 **The Behavioural Inattention Test (BIT) breakfast tray task**
This contains items that examine for the possibility of visual neglect in real-world-type tasks. In one example, a large card with a picture of a breakfast tray on it is placed before the patient. The patient is then asked to describe what is on the breakfast tray. In this illustration, a patient with left neglect might well fail to mention the fried egg and baked beans on the left side of the plate.

typically describe items from only one side of the plate (mirroring the real-life observation on acute hospital wards that such patients often only eat items from one side of their plate). This issue will be covered in depth in Chapter 5.

Thus it can be seen that neuropsychological assessment of attention has made considerable progress over the last 10 years, with the development of specialist tests and batteries designed to assess these functions in theoretically derived ways. At the same time there has been a trend towards making tasks more plausible and less abstract, to enhance functional relevance (although the extent to which this is achieved in each individual test is highly debatable). At the moment, many clinicians use these tests as an add-on, i.e. something else they might do after administering a full WAIS. This no doubt reflects in part the conservatism of the profession and a reluctance to move away from a core skill that many learned soon after graduating. However, increasingly sophisticated tests across all functional domains will eventually force a change. People will seek to take advantage of what is available without requiring patients to sit through ever longer testing sessions. It is also likely that one or more of the psychological publishers will seek to further take advantage of their portfolios by taking the best from a range of their specialist batteries to derive a new general battery. We will then arrive at something akin to the WAIS but using theoretically derived tasks in clear functional domains.

Summary

This chapter has shown how clinicians have traditionally relied upon the WAIS as a core battery when conducting neuropsychological assessments but have also added in their clinical observations and results from other tests thought to be useful in this domain. It was suggested that while the WAIS does serve a useful purpose as a general screening tool, it frequently has to be supplemented to reach an adequate interpretation.

In recent years, specialist batteries of tests have been developed to assess functioning in this domain. The tests in such batteries tend to be theoretically derived, and often an attempt is made to enhance ecological validity. It is suggested that in future, clinical practice may shift more towards such an approach. There may be less reliance on a core general purpose battery. This would be facilitated by the development of a shorter screening tool to point the way towards more extensive assessments in particular domains. An alternative would be to construct a new general purpose battery from the newer more theoretically derived tests.

We have now covered the important aspects of cognitive theories of attention, considered the nature of neuropsychology and some of the more sophisticated techniques employed with patients, and are familiar with the main tests being used by clinicians and researchers to assess attention. We are now ready to go on and consider the research findings in relation to the neuropsychology of attention. We will start this with the topic of speed of processing, a notion that some have suggested can account for many apparent attentional deficits. We will then go on to consider selection, control, and vigilance.

Chapter 4

Speed of processing—an all-encompass-ing deficit

Overview

THIS CHAPTER INTRODUCES the notion of speed of processing. This is the idea that the brain can manipulate information at
a given rate, and that this rate can be changed following neurological
insult. It may seem odd to some readers to take this topic first as we
begin our exploration of the neuropsychology of attention. After all,
speed of processing is rarely if ever discussed as a topic linked to
attention in general cognitive psychology textbooks. However, in the
neuropsychological literature there has been a long-standing suggestion that reduced speed of processing in some patients can produce
behavioural deficits that are readily apparent on tests thought to tap
into attention. Thus it has been said that apparent attention deficits
may not really be due to damage to attention processes within the
brain but to an overall change in the speed with which the brain is able
to process information. In fact, some have gone so far as to suggest
that all apparent deficits in the domain of attention could be due to
this change in brain processing speed. Whether deficits in attention
really exist, or whether they are actually due to these changes in
brain processing speed, is a fairly fundamental issue in the neuropsychological literature. As such it seems appropriate to consider this
issue at the outset.

The concept is first of all described, and evidence that speed
of processing deficits are a core aspect of traumatic brain injury is
presented. Some problems with the concept are then discussed. In
particular it is suggested that the use of the concept as an all encompassing explanation for a wide range of deficits may be too convenient
and that such suggestions may be limiting more in-depth analyses. The
chapter then goes on to consider the condition of multiple sclerosis,
where slowing of mental processes may be the primary neuropsychological consequence, before reviewing a number of other conditions in which mental speed is affected. Finally, it is suggested that
precise measures of central speed, such as reaction time, are hard for
the lay person to manipulate and as such may be good measures of
malingering.

Introduction

All activities that we carry out in life take time. If we have to read and comprehend a chapter from a book, perhaps as part of a school homework assignment, it will take time. If we need to work out some figures, perhaps to complete a tax assessment, it will take time. The time taken to complete an activity will vary, depending on how complex the problem is and how much material has to be dealt with. Solving a complex jigsaw puzzle could take months, and people frequently take similarly long periods of time to complete games of chess carried out at a distance. Using the remote control to change channels on the television by comparison is a relatively quick exercise. How fast we are able to carry out such tasks is often completely inconsequential in terms of impact upon our lives. For example, it does not matter too much if we take all day to solve a difficult crossword puzzle. On other occasions the speed with which we can operate can be crucial. When driving a car, how fast we can react to someone stepping into the road can make the difference between life and death for the pedestrian involved. It is easy to see that if our reaction time when driving is impaired, this could have important consequences (Brouwer, Withaar, Tant, & van Zomeren, 2002).

The time it takes people to complete tasks such as those described above will also differ from one person to another. Such differences could be related to individual differences in ability or perhaps age (e.g. Fisk & Warr, 1996). It is beyond the scope of the current chapter to review such possibilities. What is clearly within our remit is the notion that neurological conditions may affect the speed with which an individual is able to process information.

This speed, typically referred to as "speed of information processing", is put forward as one factor affecting performance on a wide variety of tasks in the literature. For example, Ponsford and Kinsella (1992) maintain that reduced speed of processing is a pervasive deficit in head injury and that performance on a number of tasks will be impaired by such a deficit. Examples they give include symbol digit modalities, simple and choice reaction time, and both colour naming and word reading from the Stroop task (details of some of these were given in Chapter 3). It seems, therefore, that any timed task that requires a person to make some judgement in response to information can be seen as measuring speed of processing. It has long been recognized that patients with head injuries can have problems with such tasks. For example Comerford, Geffen, May, Medland, and Geffen (2002) found that patients with mild head injury were slower to judge sentences (e.g. deciding whether "nuns grow on trees" is a sensible statement).

Speed of processing deficits in head injury

The Dutch psychologist van Zomeren made an early contribution to this area with the observation that choice reaction time is impaired following head injury, and the impairment is linked to severity of the injury. Van Zomeren and Deelman (1978) further described how simple reaction time is also impaired following head injury, but with less sensitivity than choice reaction time. Both measures were, however, able to discriminate between mild, moderate, and severe injuries. Reaction time is a basic measure that has been used as a tool by psychologists throughout the recent history of cognitive theorizing. It is, as the name suggests, simply the time taken in milliseconds for a participant to respond by pressing a button when a single stimulus is presented. Typically, such stimuli are nowadays presented on a computer screen using special software to record the response times. As such, simple reaction time reflects the speed with which a person can detect a stimulus and respond. Note that no processing is required beyond that involved in detecting the stimulus and making the response. If the stimulus is a word and the person is trying hard to respond as fast as possible, he or she may not even be aware of what the word said (although he or she will generally become aware of the word since reading is a very fast and automatic process). Henderson and Dittrich (1998) pointed out that simple reaction time also includes an element of arousal, i.e. the person mentally coils him-/herself up ready to spring when the stimulus appears. They presented evidence that some patients are impaired in this aspect. Thus we should not underestimate the humble simple reaction time task and its ability to provide useful information about patients.

Choice reaction time is more complex and requires the participant to process the stimuli in order to decide which response to make. For example, the person may be asked to respond by pressing one button if the stimulus is a green square, or another button if the stimulus is a red circle. In each case the person needs to process the stimulus to identify the relevant features and make the decision as to which button to press. In van Zomeren and Deelman's (1978) study, choice reaction time was noted to be more sensitive to different degrees of injury than simple reaction time. This suggests that the additional cognitive processes involved in the former are more vulnerable to the effects of injury than the simpler target detection and unitary responding involved the latter. Thus a generalized speed of processing deficit may impact differently on different processes, perhaps depending upon their complexity or the number of processing stages involved.

Despite these early results, simple and choice reaction times are not routinely assessed by clinical psychologists. Collins and Long (1996) suggested that such measures could usefully be added to the typical assessment regime. They found that measures of simple and choice reaction time were often impaired in head injury even when other measures, such as the subtests from the Halstead–Reitan neuropsychological test battery, were unaffected.

It therefore seems that the speed with which we can process information is a common deficit in head injuries, even in very mild cases. For example, Hinton-Byre, Geffen, and McFarland (1997) found that immediately after sustaining mild concussion, rugby players were slower to comprehend a list of sentences.

Does the speed of processing decrement explain other deficits?

Brouwer, Ponds, van Wolffelaar, and van Zomeren (1989) were interested in the extent to which patients would be impaired in their ability to drive if they were not able to perform a dual task. Driving is a complex skill, which requires the successful co-ordination of a number of activities. If we are unable to attend adequately to the road ahead at the same time as monitoring the position of the car and engine speed, then we will have problems. In their procedure, Brouwer and colleagues looked at the ability of patients to combine tasks in a simulated driving scenario. Before doing the task, they determined each patient's ability to carry out the two elements independently, and then adjusted the difficulty according to this. What they found was that when allowance was made for the patients' reduced ability to perform each task alone, there was no dual task deficit when the tasks were combined, over and above that observed in the controls. The authors therefore suggest that the difficulty patients with head injury typically experience in carrying out dual tasks is due to their decreased speed of processing. There is no specific "dual task" deficit, for example in the control processes (often referred to as the central executive; see Chapter 6).

Later studies (e.g. Veltman, Brouwer, van Zomeren, & van Wolffelaar, 1996) made a similar point with respect to executive functions and planning. More recently, the same argument was advanced by Crawford, Bryan, Luszcz, Obonsawin, and Stewart (2000). This study looked at a large sample of data collected with the Weschler Adult Intelligence Scale (WAIS; see Chapter 3). A number of the tests included in this battery are said to measure "executive" functions, i.e. the ability to concentrate and plan a sequence of steps to achieve a complex goal on a novel task. Probably the best example of this is the Block Design task. In this test the person being examined is given a set of coloured blocks, the sides of which can be red, white, or both. Using the blocks the participant has to make up a complex design (Figure 3.1).

Crawford et al. argued that although some people in their sample had "executive" deficits, these problems tended to correlate with performance on the Digit Symbol task (see Chapter 3), which requires participants to copy symbols from a key into a grid containing a random sequence of numbers. It is thought to measure a number of processes, including manual dexterity, speed, concentration, attention, and memory. Given the heavy speed component, it is often taken as an index of speed of processing. Thus, because "executive" deficits correlated with difficulties on the Digit Symbol task, Crawford et al. argued that the "executive" deficits were not necessarily real but simply a consequence of the slow speed of processing.

What each of these studies seems to be suggesting is that speed of processing can be conceived of as a general system property. Just as with the modern desktop computer, which has a set speed of operation that depends on how advanced the central processing chip is, the brain as a whole processes information at a particular speed. This overall system property is said to be decreased in some conditions (particularly head injury). Thus all of the brain processes will be slowed down, leading to patients having difficulties on a range of tasks. They might not be able to dual task or solve problems, and fatigue easier, leading to apparent vigilance decrements. While each of these problems can appear to be quite different in nature, they all arise from the same source: they are all a consequence of slow speed of processing. Thus the head injured patient cannot be said to have an "executive" deficit, the problem really arose from slow speed of information processing.

Such a suggestion is very seductive. It appears to have a great appeal in terms of parsimony, in other words many of the problems experienced by head-injured clients could be explained in terms of this relatively straightforward concept. Perhaps all the attention deficits identified in patients could be a consequence of this global change in a fundamental system property of the brain. Unfortunately, it is the current author's view that such an explanation will turn out to be simply too convenient.

The problem with the notion of "speed of information processing" is that it may be too simplistic to assume that there is such a convenient general system property of the brain. As such, the concept seems to suggest that all speeded tasks are capable of tapping into this fundamental brain process to a similar extent. What has not been addressed is whether certain tasks are more likely to be impacted by changes in brain processing speed compared to others, or whether different tasks may even be processed at different rates by different parts of the brain. Psychologists often make a distinction between controlled and automatic processes. Controlled processing requires conscious energy while automatic processes are over learned and take place with little overt mental effort. For example, if we are trying to solve a novel and original puzzle it may require considerable thought, whereas a skilled cyclist need not worry too much about maintaining his or her balance as they pedal along. It may be the case that controlled processes are more likely to be affected by changes in brain speed, whereas automatic processing is less so. If we accept that the brain accomplishes processing through the activation of networks of neurons, one might envisage that some processes involve very large and complex networks that may take longer to resolve than smaller networks that accomplish simpler tasks. More complex tasks may require a sequence of networks to accomplish them, again leading to a longer processing time. In short, there is no reason to suppose that speed of processing as a variable affects all processes in the same kind of way, or that all processes operate with the same degree of efficiency. A computer analogy might be helpful here. For most modern computers, the operation of most processes is governed by the speed of the central processing chip, nowadays typically running at several giga Hertz (GHz). Thus all software operating on the computer has a limitation imposed by the speed of the central chip. However, not all software will make use of that processing capacity with the same degree of efficiency. It is possible, for example, that several different word processing programs will accomplish key tasks at different speeds. Furthermore, for some processes speed rates vary because the operation of other chips comes into play. Graphics programs typically make use of a dedicated graphics chip, which may run at a different speed to the central chip. Coming back to the brain, it may be the case that the frontal lobes, carrying out an overall co-ordination role, typically accomplish their processes at a different rate to the occipital lobes dealing with vision.

Not all studies take the view that speed of information processing deficits can account for other problems. Azouvi, Jokic, van der Linden, and Marlier (1996) for example, suggested that speed could not totally account for planning deficits they observed in patients. Bate, Matthias, and Crawford (2001) pointed out that while patients with traumatic brain injury did show slowing, they did not have problems on Posner's Test of Covert Orientation of Attention (see Figure 1.7). This indicates that the ability to direct one's attention around the visual field, engaging and disengaging targets as necessary, is not as dependent on speed of information processing.

If one is not waylaid by the all encompassing speed of processing view, a more complex analysis of attention is possible. For example,

Schmitter-Edgecomb and Roger (1997) conducted a thorough study in which patients with closed head injury were compared with controls (i.e. patients without head injury) in their abilities to perform a categorization task over a large number of trials. In one condition, consistent mappings were evident in the stimuli, giving the participants the opportunity to learn the stimuli set and increase their speed of responding. Thus the participants might be told to always press the right button if a green square appeared, and the left button for a red circle. Eventually under these conditions performance becomes very fast, and can be said to have been automated. In the second condition, stimuli mappings were constantly varied. For a few trials the participants might be told to press the right button for a green square and the left for a red circle, but after a while they might be told to do the opposite, or given a new set of directions. Hence there was less chance of improvement, and performance in this condition remained slow and stable. In the consistent mapping condition, the patients with closed head injury improved their performance in a similar fashion to controls, but the rate of improvement was slower and the final speed achieved was less. In the varied mapping condition, performance of the patients with closed head injury was considerably slower throughout, with no group showing improvement. What this study illustrates is that patients with closed head injury are able to automate their performance. The eventual performance achieved is slower than that of the control group, reflecting the overall speed of processing deficit, but the difference is much less than on the varied mapping condition, where much greater levels of "controlled" processing are required. Thus it seems that slowed speed of processing is more evident on tasks which are said to require large amounts of controlled processing, but much less evident on tasks with high degrees of automation.

According to the view being expressed in the above paragraph, to claim, as Crawford et al. (2000) and Veltman et al. (1996) do, that "executive" deficits are fully explained by the speed of processing decrement, may be somewhat misleading and direct attention away from an important aspect of these patients' behaviour. This all-encompassing speed of processing deficit hypothesis seems to suggest that decreased performance on executive tasks is simply due to the speed at which the relevant planning and problem solving can be carried out. The possibility that frontal networks may be particularly adversely affected by whatever pathology causes general speed decrements, thus making it harder for them to resolve and process information cleanly, seems to be discounted. Furthermore, when researchers refer to speed of processing, the tasks used often involve a high degree of "controlled" processing. Tasks such as sentence comprehension, complex reaction time, etc., require a high degree of attention and concentration. A purer measure of speed would be simple reaction time, also known to be impaired but to a lesser degree and with less sensitivity. Thus an element of "executive processing" is built in to most measures of speed of processing. It is not surprising, therefore, that when we control for the speed of processing measures, deficits on executive measures appear to be accounted for. Nevertheless, it is important and interesting that, for whatever reason, the patient has difficulties on "executive" tasks. It is also important and interesting that this deficit may be less apparent in automated tasks and that patients are still capable of achieving such automation. The area of functioning most affected by a decline in brain speed may be the executive or control functions, and whatever their aetiology, either specific frontal brain lesions or system-wide declines in brain speed, they are likely to be of key importance in determining a patient's abilities to carry out the functions of daily living. Another way of phrasing the objection to the "all encompassing speed of processing view" in this paragraph is to suggest that what we mean by speed of processing may really be speed of controlled processing, and this may be independent of other brain functions such as automatization and vigilance.

One final piece of evidence will be referred to on this issue. Robertson, Ward, Ridgeway, and Nimmo-Smith (1996) presented a large normative data set on number of indices of attentional functioning, collected during the norming of the Test of Everyday Attention (TEA). This included measures of the key theoretical constructs in attention, including visual and auditory selection, attention switching, and vigilance. The factor analysis (see Glossary) of the data revealed a three-factor solution. The first factor included mainly measures of selection, many of which involved speeded performance. Other factors reflected attention switching and vigilance. The fact that a number of distinct factors appeared seems to argue that not all processes are underpinned to a significant degree by processing speed. In the normal population, vigilance at least is independent of the speed at which we can operate (vigilance here means the ability to maintain an alert state and detect occasional targets over a period of 10 minutes, as on the TEA lottery ticket task).

To summarize the preceding discussion. A slowing of brain speed appears to be a ubiquitous consequence of traumatic brain injury, even in very mild injuries occasioned during the pursuit of rugby. This change in a basic system property of the brain is probably indexed by simple reaction time tasks, but the consequences are even more evident on more complex tasks, presumably because these involve more processing stages. Thus controlled processes are especially affected, while automatic processes are less affected. It has been suggested here that executive processes may be the most vulnerable of all to this decline in speed of processing, and it does not make sense to treat this as some kind of "pseudo" executive deficit. Exactly what we mean by "speed of processing" needs to be further refined, and the precise mechanisms by which various processes are affected more fully explained. Is it that processes simply execute more slowly, or are the operating characteristics of processes changed by the pathology in a much more complex and as yet undetermined way? At the same time, researchers should fully explore the implications of a speed of processing deficit for all aspects of functioning, determining for example to what extent selection and vigilance might be affected or spared. Few studies with patients have as yet have included sound measures of vigilance alongside speed of processing measures.

Speed of processing in other conditions

Given that white matter changes have been put forward as a mechanism underlying changes in speed of processing (Ylikoski, Ylikoski, Erkinjuntti, & Sulkava, 1993), it is no surprise that head-injured patients experience this difficulty, given the extensive white matter shearing that takes place in severe head trauma. We would also expect other conditions that produce change in the white matter to result in this difficulty. One condition that confirms this prediction is multiple sclerosis.

Multiple sclerosis

Multiple sclerosis is an autoimmune disease that causes extensive demyelination of peripheral neurons and may result in central white matter changes. It has been suggested that speed of information processing may be the key deficit in this condition (Demaree, DeLuca, Gaudino, & Diamond, 1999). Archibald and Fisk (2000) suggested that the speed deficit is apparent early in the disease course, whereas additional deficits in working memory appear later on as the disease progresses. Rao, St Aubin Faubert, and Leo (1989) report decreased reaction time and scanning time in a task based on Sternberg's paradigm. In this task, participants are given a set of numbers that they have to keep in mind, e.g. 6, 2, 9. They then see a random sequence of the digits 1 to 9 presented on a screen. Each time a number that matches one of those they are keeping in mind appears they have to respond by pressing a particular key. Reaction time increases as the number of items held in mind increases, and one can work out the scanning time by comparing the single number instance (i.e. holding in mind one number, e.g. 2) with the multiple digit instance (e.g. holding in mind 5, 2, 7, say). If the reaction times between the single-digit instance and the three-digit instance are, say, 300 and 360 ms, then the cost of scanning the three digits in the more complex condition can be said to be 60 ms. Thus Rao et al. have shown that the reduced performance in their patients with multiple sclerosis was not just due to peripheral slowing, as some might have suggested given the peripheral demyelination of neurons. Rather, there appears to be a central component as well, due to the slowing of scanning speed (which can be conceived as reflecting central processes). In other words, deficits in multiple sclerosis probably reflect the involvement of neurons in the brain as well as neurons in the peripheral tissues.

As with head injury, this speed deficit appears to cause difficulties on complex tasks such as dual tasking (D'Esposito et al., 1996), which correlates with performance on the Paced Auditory Serial Addition task. Planning deficits on the Tower of Hanoi have also been found (Arnett et al., 1997) (see Figure 1.10 and descriptions in Chapter 3).

Given the hypothesized centrality of speed of processing deficits in multiple sclerosis, it is not surprising that a popular measure of speed, the Paced Auditory Serial Additions task (PASAT) has been put forward by workers and special interest groups as a key outcome measure to be included in studies of the condition (Snyder, Capelleri, Archibald, & Fisk, 2001).

The PASAT has been in use in neuropsychology for several decades (e.g. Gronwall, 1977) and is widely accepted as a measure of speed of information processing. The task is fully described in Chapter 3. Scores on the test typically reflect the number of times the testee correctly shouts out the sum of the successive pairs of stimuli, giving a maximum score of 59 for a typical sequence of 60 numbers. Snyder et al. suggest that the PASAT is more sensitive if scored on the basis of correct dyads only, as this avoids the possibility of strategy use, which can confound the traditional scoring method with participants who are not scoring well. In other words, if we are really struggling at the task, then the temptation is to shout out the answers only for every other pair of numbers, and thus avoid the confusion of trying to get every possible successive pair. With Snyder et al.'s method of scoring, credit is only received for correct answers that follow an immediately proceeding correct answer, thus eliminating the benefits of adopting a partial report strategy.

While the PASAT may prove to be a useful measure for use in multiple sclerosis, especially with Snyder et al.'s modified scoring criteria, a note of caution needs to be mentioned with respect to this task. The assumption underlying the PASAT is that most adults who learned their number bonds well in school (i.e. simple arithmetic facts such as $2 + 4 = 6$) can retrieve such information in a fairly effortless and automatic way. Thus impairment on the PASAT reflects an inability to deal fast enough with the incoming information, not an inability to carry out the simple arithmetic involved. A recent study (Ward, 1997) questioned this assumption. In this study, a group of university students was found to score significantly worse on the PASAT than a group of healthy, community-dwelling elderly persons matched for IQ. This seems to suggest that the ability to carry out the simple arithmetic involved in the PASAT has changed across these cohorts, perhaps due to generational changes in pedagogical practice (few people would support the other possibility, that the younger students have a slower rate of information processing—we are generally thought to slow down with age). Certainly in the past there seems to have been more emphasis placed, in early years education, on the recitation of simple arithmetic facts. Anyone who doubts this change can convince themselves quite easily with the following test. Stop at random a selection of young people, say under 30 years old, and ask them, without warning, to tell you what 8 X 7 is. Then stop a random number of people over 60 and give them the same task. In my experience most 60-plus-year-olds perform the task easily, while I have known even university students either to be unable to give a response or resort to using their fingers! Thus there is a problem in seeing the PASAT as a pure measure of speed of information processing, since arithmetic fact retrieval is also involved. Neither can this problem simply be overcome by using different norms for the younger generation, since within the younger cohort there are wide discrepancies in number fact retrieval ability. Those who went to "old fashioned" schools that practice extensive number fact retrieval in the early years will fare relatively better. Thus this skill is unevenly distributed within the younger population, rendering the PASAT an invalid measure of speed of information processing. (Note that there is no criticism of modern educational practices here—small children may benefit far more from engaging in creative activities than from spending hours on rote rehearsal, especially now that calculators are widely available.)

Other conditions

Speed of processing deficits have been put forward as features of a wide variety of other conditions. The latest version of the WAIS includes a number of tasks that are thought to include basic perceptual processing, e.g. detecting differences in quite similar patterns in the Matrices task. Scores from these various tasks can be combined to produce an overall perceptual speed factor score. Dickinson and Coursey (2002) suggest this perceptual speed factor is a good predictor of community functioning in schizophrenic patients, although the role of medication needs to be considered. Inspection time is the length of time a person has to look at a display to make some perceptual judgement, e.g. in deciding which of two presented lines is longer. Tsourtos, Thompson, and Stough (2002) found that patients with unmedicated depression were slower on an inspection time task than either controls or medicated patients.

Attention deficit hyperactivity disorder is a condition that is being increasingly identified in children. The affected children are unable to concentrate, are highly distractible, and often find it difficult to sit still. A number of studies (Hynd, Nieves, Connor, & Stone, 1989; Johnston, Hogg, Schopp, Kapila, & Edwards, 2002; Myerson, Lawrence, Hale, Jenkins, & Chen, 1998; Weiler, Holmes Bernstein, Bellinger, & Waber, 2000) suggest that speed of processing deficits exist in attention deficit hyperactivity disorder (see Chapter 6 for discussion of control in this condition), although the role of concomitant reading problems and hyperactivity needs to be explored in more detail.

Cardiac surgery may impact on processing speed (Williams, LeMarche, Alexander, & Stanford 1996) as may hypoglycaemia (Driesen, Cox, Gonder-Frederick, & Clarke, 1995) and presymptomatic infection with human immunodeficiency virus (HIV) (Hart, Wade, Klinger, & Hamer, 1990). Finally, Michiels, de Gucht, Cluydts, & Fischler (1999) suggested that slow speed of information processing was present in chronic fatigue syndrome (CFS) and was not linked to other attention deficits, although Vercoulen et al. (1998) suggested that few of their patients were slowed and those that were had reduced physical activity. CFS is a difficult disorder, which has often produced lively discussion about its basis and underlying deficits. This leads on to the next section.

Malingering and speed of processing

This short section is based on ongoing work in collaboration with the University of the West Indies. We have developed a computerized neuropsychological screening battery (Ward, 2002), which is intended for use in screening neurological patients at the various health centres on the island of Jamaica. Using this battery in a recent study of CFS patients, we found some interesting anomalies in the data. CFS patients report fatigue, and quite often impaired sleep patterns. However, they retain an otherwise intact neuropsychological profile, i.e. there are no deficits in memory or attention. We found that some of our patients in the CFS study apparently had gross deficits on simple and choice reaction time, as well as on other speeded measures. This was surprising. In fact the deficits displayed by about 5% of our sample were worse than those observed by moderately demented patients, a group with a considerably worse overall pattern of neuropsychological functioning. On closer examination it became apparent that a number of these patients had simple reaction times considerably worse than their choice reaction times. Trying to explain such a pattern is a theoretical challenge that seems to require an explanation outside the domain of cognitive function. In short, we are left with the impression that a small percentage of patients with CFS are very concerned that their condition should be verified by the existence of performance deficits on psychometric tests. They therefore attempt to manipulate their performance, but the result of this is a highly unlikely pattern across tests.

Since the early days of exploration in this domain, psychologists have used measures of simple and choice reaction time (e.g. van Zomeren & Deelman, 1978). Such measures are difficult for the typical patient to conceive. In a simple reaction time task, the participant has to press a button as soon as a single stimulus is presented. In choice reaction time, a number of buttons are specified, depending on which of several stimuli is presented. Simple reaction time is typically, in our experience, of the order of around 240 ms in young (i.e. 18- to 35-year-old) participants, while two choice reaction time is typically 100 ms slower, at around 340 ms. Simple reaction time is always slower than choice reaction time in motivated participants who understand the task requirements. The average man in the street would not know these figures and would not necessarily realize the theoretical relatedness of simple and choice reaction time. It is impossible for someone trying to manipulate their performance to systematically alter their responding on the simple reaction time task in any kind of credible way. People might, for example, attempt to delay each response slightly, perhaps by saying the word "and" to themselves before pressing the key. Such attempts at manipulation will, however, result in data way outside the normal expectation. To be credible, a patient would need to bring their reaction time down by about 40–80 ms. The only way to achieve this would be for a statistically sophisticated client to realize that a credible overall reaction time, within the impaired range, will be achieved by dropping performance on a small percentage of trials and responding normally on the rest. However, such attempts could easily be dealt with by the use of outlier techniques, e.g. rejecting from the calculation of mean reaction time any trials that are more than 2 standard deviations from the mean. Furthermore, few clients will realize the significance of a simple reaction time that is slower than choice reaction time, such that an attempt at manipulation will result in a simple reaction time that is either slower or proportionally too close to the choice reaction time.

We are currently further exploring the use of simple and choice reaction time alongside other measures of speed of processing as indices of malingered performance. Such measures could usefully be incorporated into assessment regimes, especially where compensation or other such issues are at stake. Of course, as with any malingering detection strategy, a genuine performance on such tasks will not validate poor performance on other tests. A client setting out to present a pattern of deficit will probably perform according to his or her own preconceived notions of what deficits might be reasonable given a particular condition (the malingering literature might benefit from considering the illness representation approach as a guide to where particular patient groups might be expected to under perform). However, making it known to clients that such objective and difficult-to-manipulate measures are going to be used in an assessment might motivate some to give a clear pattern of performance throughout. All of this, of course, does not detract from the use of such measures in head injury as a key indicator of a significant and pervasive deficit capable of giving an index of the clients current recovery of function— that of speed of information processing.

Summary

In this chapter we have seen that the concept "speed of processing" has become widely used in neuropsychology, although it has not been precisely defined and a wide range of measures have been put forward as reflecting this system property of the brain. Clearly, a pervasive deficit in traumatic brain injury slows down the rate at which people can accomplish cognitive tasks. However, it is unclear if all brain processes are equally affected or whether some domains are especially vulnerable. In particular, controlled, as opposed to automated, processes may be particularly susceptible. Multiple sclerosis is a condition in which speed of processing is being put forward as the primary deficit. In reflection of this, a widely used test of speed of processing, the PASAT, is being suggested as a key outcome measure for this condition, although the validity of this particular measure has been questioned. A number of conditions are said to affect speed of processing and it is possible that measures of speed that give fine-grained data such as simple and choice reaction time are difficult for patients to manipulate and could be useful for the detection of malingering in contested cases.

Chapter 5

Selective attention

Overview

THIS CHAPTER REVIEWS the neuropsychological findings with respect to selective attention. Although there have been quite a number of studies on this topic, it is probably fair to say at the current time that the effort has not been particularly systematic. No standard techniques have been used to thoroughly assess in particular conditions how this function breaks down. There are, however some exceptions to this. For example, Posner's (e.g. Posner, Walker, Friedrich, & Rafal, 1984) method of looking at the effect of valid and invalid cueing in visual attention has been widely used to examine performance in a number of conditions (see Chapter 1 for outline of Posner's methodology). Also, the striking condition known as unilateral visual neglect has received much attention, perhaps because it is relatively common in patients following stroke and potentially quite incapacitating. A range of theories have been put forward to account for the phenomena.

This chapter commences with a brief review of some of the clearer studies that have attempted to localize functions in selective attention, all of which look at the visual domain. Then studies that have looked at particular conditions will be surveyed, including Alzheimer's disease, schizophrenia, and head injury. Finally, the phenomenon of unilateral neglect will be outlined and the theories put forward to account for it discussed.

Pointers to localization of selective visual attention

Modern neurophysiological methods used to try and determine where in the brain particular processes are located are quite varied (see Chapter 2). The following section describes research that has used some of those techniques and it might be worth looking back at the end of Chapter 2 to remind yourself what some of those techniques are. Also, to help locate some of the major brain regions mentioned, a simplified brain diagram is provided here (Figure 5.1).

Le Tuong, Pardo, and Hu (1998) used functional magnetic resonance imaging (fMRI) to determine that parietal and cerebellar

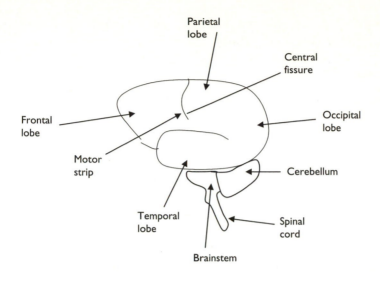

Figure 5.1 **A simplified lateral view of the cerebral cortex, showing major regions and structures**

areas are implicated in the shifting of visual attention. Mangun, Hopfinger, Kussmaul, Fletcher, & Heinze (1997) used event-related potentials (ERPs) and positron emission tomography (PET) to conclude that ventral and lateral extrastriate areas are involved in selective attention, a finding also supported by Hillyard et al. (1997). A previous study by Heinze, Mangun, Burchert, & Hinrichs (1994) also implicated the extrastriate visual cortex, with right hemisphere activation when a target was on the left and vice versa for a target on the right. Fink et al. (1996) suggested that tempo-parietal areas are involved in change of focus (i.e. moving from looking at an object to focusing on a particular feature) whereas the prestriate area was involved in visual selection.

From the previous discussion, it appears that extrastriate cortex is important in visual selection as are the parietal lobes. Such findings are in agreement with the "two cortical visual systems" hypothesis of Ungerleider and Mishkin (1982). These authors proposed an occipital–parietal–frontal circuit for dealing with spatial representation and an occipital–temporal–frontal circuit for processing object identity. This spatial pathway, involving the parietal lobes, will be revisited in the later discussion of unilateral neglect.

Selective attention deficits in patients

Alzheimer's disease

Since Alzheimer's disease (AD) pathology is widely distributed in the brain, particularly in the parietal and temporal lobes, it would not be surprising to find that selective attention deficits can be an early and prominent feature of the condition. Such deficits are likely to prove highly disruptive to patients, with Duchek, Hunt, Ball, and Buckles (1997) suggesting that many patients may not be safe to drive. This is largely as a consequence of selective attention deficits causing them not to pay attention to important features of the driving situation and to be easily distracted by unimportant aspects. Parasuraman and Nestor had similar findings (1991). Further, Simone and Baylis (1997) found that their sample of patients with AD were subject to massive interference from distracters in a reaching task. Langley, Overmier, Knopman, and Prod'Homme (1998) asked participants to read a list of letters under one of three different conditions in which each letter was presented alongside a distracter (Figure 5.2). Patients were significantly more distracted than controls but there was no difference between negative priming and habituation conditions.

This distractibility was further demonstrated in an elegant study by Grande, McGlinchey-Berroth, Milberg, and D'Esposito (1996). In this study, patients were shown two pictures, one above the other, and asked to attend to the top-most picture (Figure 5.3). This was immediately followed by a word, which they had to read. If the attended picture is a representation of the word, then the word will be read faster, a phenomenon known as identity priming. The unattended picture, however, should produce no such effect, because it is being ignored. This was what was observed in the control group. Interestingly, though, in patients with AD the ignored picture produced positive priming if it was a representation of the subsequent word. Thus patients with AD appear to be incapable of selectively attending

Distraction condition.

A   S

Y   P

G   W

D   P

Q   N

Habituation condition

L   F

W   P

H   F

C   W

Negative priming condition

D   Y

Y   Q

Q   I

I   P

P   W

Figure 5.2 **Langley et al.'s procedure**
In each condition the task is to read out the letters presented on the left. In the distraction condition, random letters presented simultaneously on the right act as distracters. In the habituation condition, a repeating sequence of letters is used as distraction, so participants become relatively less distracted. In the negative priming condition, the distracter on one trial becomes the target on the immediately following trial, which should lead to a slowing in response time as the stimuli was previously subject to inhibition.

85

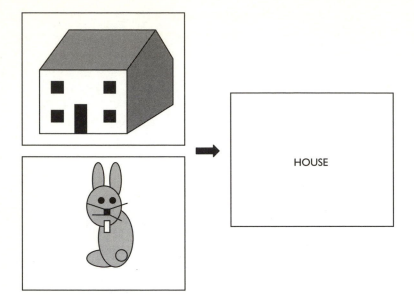

Figure 5.3 **Grande et al.'s experiment**
The participant has to name the top picture, e.g. house. If this is immediately followed by the same word, e.g. "house", then that word is named much quicker. In patients with Alzheimer's disease, if the word is related to the ignored picture, it is also named quicker, e.g. if the word "carrot" were presented in the illustration. Thus patients with Alzheimer's disease were unable to ignore the lower picture.

only to the upper-most picture. They are distracted by the lower picture, processing it to the extent that it then produces a positive priming effect to the subsequent word.

This inability to direct spatial attention was further illustrated by Parasuraman, Greenwood, and Alexander (1995), who asked patients to perform a single feature search (e.g. looking for a square) and a dual feature search (e.g. looking for a red square) and provided prominent spatial cues. Patients with AD did not appear to be able to benefit from the spatial cues. More recently, Parasuraman, Greenwood, and Alexander (2000) suggested that patients with AD could only benefit from precise orientation cues and Coslett, et al. (1995) reported two cases who seemed to have a reduced attentional spotlight.

By contrast, Caffarra, Riggio, Malvezzi, Scaglioni, and Freedman (1997) suggested that AD patients did not appear to have a deficit in disengagement on the Posner paradigm (see Chapter 1 for a description of how disengagement can be manipulated on a simple visual task).

Finally, Amieva, Lafont, Dartigues, and Fabrigoule (1999), pointed out that in a visual search task, commission errors were increased where distracters shared features with targets. Thus patients with AD also have an inability to inhibit distracters. Recently, Gainotti, Marra, and Villa (2001) reported that patients with AD were worse on the detection of visual targets with multiple features than patients with multi-infarct dementia.

In recent years, the condition of Lewy body dementia (LBD) has been differentiated from AD (McKeith, Fairbairn, Briel, & Harrison, 1993). LBD has a distinct pathology, consisting of Lewy bodies, often concentrated in the frontal and temporal regions of the brain. Lewy bodies are abnormal structures that appear in the brains of patients as a result of the degeneration of brain tissue. In the same way, AD is distinguished by the presence of neurofibrillary tangles and senile plaques, formed as a result of neuronal loss. It has been suggested that patients with LBD tend to have greater attentional disturbance than patients with AD. For example, Sahgal, Galloway, McKeith, and Edwardson (1992) found that visual search was worse in LBD than AD. Calderon et al. (2001), in a careful and detailed study, reported that whereas AD patients have impaired selective attention, LBD patients have greater impairments, and also show considerable deficits in other aspects of attention.

Thus patients with AD seem to have problems focusing their visual attention, being easily influenced by distracters, and the effective scope of their attentional focus may be much reduced. It seems likely that patients with LBD may have even more pronounced and striking deficits in these areas.

Schizophrenia

Of all the mental illnesses, schizophrenia is undoubtedly the one that arouses the most interest amongst students. Unlike depression and anxiety disorders, which can be seen as representing extremes of mood that all of us can relate to in a milder form, schizophrenia involves phenomena outside normal day-to-day experience. The most striking such aspect is the phenomena of auditory hallucinations, typically presenting as voices. Hearing voices in our heads is not, in fact, all that unusual. Most of us experience our train of thought as a verbal process in our head. If we introspect for a moment, and listen to our inner thought process, we might even recognize that the internal voice shares our normal vocal characteristics; it sounds like us. We can even summon up the voices of others. For example, many of us have memories of our parents, probably our mother, shouting to us as a child, e.g. "Come on in, its time for dinner", or "Come on, time to get up and get ready for school". If you close your eyes for a moment I am sure that you could imagine the sound of your mother's voice (or anyone else you know well) saying some typical phrase. So internal experience of auditory stimuli is not unusual (if you are like me, then you may often spend part of each day engaging your "mental" walkman, perhaps playing over and over again in your head the sound of some music you have been listening to lately). What makes the schizophrenic experience different and so extraordinary is that the hallucinated voices come completely out of the blue. They are experienced by the patient in exactly the same way as any real voice they might hear. Consequently, patients often look around to see who is speaking. They may come up with complex rationalizations to explain what is happening, perhaps thinking that someone has planted secret speakers in their room. I remember reading once of a submariner who was convinced that the other sailors were talking about him and that the sound of their voices was being carried along the metal piping of his submarine. The patients feel that they have no control over what the voices are saying. Often the voices will comment on what the patient is doing, or may be derogatory. Occasionally, patients report that the voices urge them to take some course of action or try to influence their decision making.

Such a strange phenomenon as hearing voices at first seems unlikely to submit to any easy explanations, but a number of theories have been proposed. One popular notion is that such patients have some kind of deficit in their attentional system, at a preconscious level.

Thus most of us are able to selectively attend to particular sounds, and filter out repetitive noise from our conscious experience. So that after a while we cease to be aware of a ticking clock or a dripping tap. However, what if some of these sounds were to penetrate that filter and work their way into our conscious mind? But because these stimuli are unattended and unsolicited, they appear in the patient's experience not as some nondescript sound, such as a dripping tap, but as a voice. The content then reflects the patient's current thoughts and concerns at that time, and thus are a reflection of his or her own thought processes. Several therapists have subscribed to such a view. If schizophrenic hallucinations are due to some kind of selective attention deficit, then we might expect to find evidence of deficits on various tasks of selective attention. Many studies have sought this elusive confirmation of the theory.

Myles-Worsley, Coon, and Byerly (1998) found that schizophrenic patients were impaired on a visual selective attention task, and Lussier and Stip (1999) found that patients could not launch an exhaustive visual search. Ward, Catts, Fox, and Michie (1991) showed that on an auditory task patients had abnormal ERPs, with a reduced P300 component. The deficits in the P300 were correlated with a measure of negative symptoms (e.g. apathy, withdrawal) and other abnormalities in the ERP were correlated with positive symptoms (e.g. thought disorder, hearing voices). Iwanami, Isono, Okajima, Noda, and Kamijima (1998) showed similar changes in the ERP during a dichotic listening task. Finally, Stip, Lussier, Lalonde, Luyet, and Fabian (1999) suggested that atypical antipsychotics, improve patient's performance on selective attention tasks. Traditional antipsychotics, such as chlorpromazine, were renowned for producing undesirable side effects such as heavy sedation. The newer "atypical" antipsychotics are more selective in the neurotransmitters they target and not only produce fewer side effects but may actually enhance cognition. The fact that the neurotransmitters targeted are in the frontal regions of the brain has led to the view that schizophrenia may be a frontal disorder, an assertion supported by Iwanami et al. (1998) in their ERP study.

A number of studies of schizophrenia seem to point towards left hemisphere deficits. For example, Wigal, Swanson, and Potkin (1997) made use of Posner's paradigm. This consists of determining the

89

extent to which stimuli appearing on either the right or left of a screen benefit from either helpful or misleading central cues (see Chapter 1 for full description). They found a right lateralized deficit on the task in medication-free schizophrenic patients; the deficit was not evident in medicated patients. Carter, Robertson, Nordahl, and Chaderjian (1996) suggested that because schizophrenic patients could not attend to the local features as opposed to global features of a stimuli, there may be a left hemisphere deficit. Carter, Robertson, Charderjian, and Celaya (1992) again hypothesized left hemisphere deficits based on the performance on Posner's task. By contrast, Oie, Rund, and Sundet (1998a) found no deficit on a dichotic listening task. The same authors did, however, report unusually rapid disengagement in Posner's paradigm (Oie, Rund, Sundet, & Bryhn, 1998b). Nestor, Faux, McCarley, and Penhune (1992) also point to disordered disengagement.

A number of studies (e.g. Brebion, Smith, Gorman, & Amador, 1996) have claimed to look at selective attention in schizophrenia using the Stroop task. In the Stroop task, patients have to shout out the colours of words while ignoring the word itself, e.g. saying "red" to the word "black" written in red ink or saying "black" to the word "red". This causes some difficulty, as words are read very quickly and effortlessly by fluent readers. It is in fact very difficult, if not impossible, for skilled readers not to read a word that is fully focused in the centre of their visual field. When we drive down the road, it is all but impossible not be aware of the messages emblazoned on roadside advertising hoardings, and as we walk through town we cannot help but be aware of the latest giveaway burger offer at the fast food joint, no matter how much we detest fast food. As such, the Stroop task is very effective. However, it is not really measuring selective attention as we traditionally conceive that skill. Selective attention typically involves searching for a target item amongst a display of distracter items. The Stroop task, however, involves attending to a particular feature of a stimulus while trying to ignore a second feature of the same stimulus. If the stimulus happens to be a word, then the word itself proves difficult to ignore, and we have to work hard to inhibit this tendency. Thus the Stroop is more usually seen as a test of inhibition, reflecting frontal lobe functioning, and these studies will therefore be considered in more detail in Chapter 6.

Thus, selective attention deficits have frequently been hypothesized in schizophrenia, using a variety of tasks and paradigms. The suggestion of specific left hemisphere deficits is a recurring theme, although not all authors agree on this aspect. How important these deficits are in the overall picture of the condition depends, in part, on how important we deem deficits found in other areas of attention in schizophrenia. These will be discussed in detail in later chapters.

Selective attention in other disorders

Schmitter-Edgecombe and Kibby (1998) found that patients with closed head injury were impaired at visual search under conditions of low discriminability and, as would be predicted from Chapter 4, they were slower. Gehring and Knight (2002) found that patients with prefrontal damage showed greater distraction from interference in choice reaction time, and that left prefrontal cortex was the most critical. Keller, Schlenker, and Pigache (1995) found that patients with closed head injury were bad at dichotic listening under fast presentation rates, while right cerebrovascular accident patients were impaired under all conditions, showing an impairment to direct their attention around the auditory space. Parkinson's patients have also been found to have selective attention deficits (Maddox, Filoteo, Delis, & Salmon, 1996).

In children, attention deficit hyperactivity disorder (ADHD) has been associated with deficits in selective attention. Jonkman, Kemner, Verbaten, and Koelega (1997) found deficits in both auditory and visual selective attention. In tasks with 10% targets, the ADHD children had fewer hits and made more false-positive responses. A hit is where a target is correctly detected, whereas a false positive is where a distracter is incorrectly responded to. The P3b component of the ERP was also reduced (ERPs and their components were described in Chapter 2).

Unilateral visual neglect

As is evident from above, research mapping out all the consequences of the many neurological conditions for selective attention is at an early stage. However, in one area there has been a great deal of interest; this is the area of unilateral neglect. For example, according to the PsychInfo database (a comprehensive database of the psychological literature), the term "unilateral neglect" has been included in over 450 publications since 1988. The actual number of studies will in fact be much higher, given that a variety of other terms have also been used to describe the condition (e.g. left neglect, hemi-inattention syndrome). Perhaps the reason for this interest has been, on the one hand, the dramatic nature of this condition and, on the other hand, the high frequency of its occurrence; it is found in a high proportion of patients following stroke.

Damage to one side of the brain often produces weakness on the opposite side of the body and, in the visual domain, patients may cease to respond to that side of space (the contralesional side). Thus patients with left hemisphere damage may ignore the right side of space (right side unilateral neglect), while right hemisphere damage leads to neglecting the left side of space (left side neglect). This phenomenon is not a result of damage to the primary visual, motor, or sensory circuits, as neglect can be observed in patients with no such deficits (Halligan, Marshall, & Wade, 1990). The neglect is often clearly evident on perceptual tasks. For example, a patient asked to cancel circles on a page will miss those to the left, while when asked to draw the detail on a clock face, all detail is put into the right hand side (Figure 5.4).

Patients often have little awareness of their deficits, which undoubtedly adds to their difficulties (Gordon & Diller, 1983). Interestingly, right visual neglect, caused by left hemisphere damage, frequently resolves quite quickly. Right neglect, however, can be very long lasting.

A condition that is related to unilateral neglect might help us to understand the condition. Damage to the occipital-parieto-frontal pathway (thought to process location information), if present bilaterally, can lead to the condition of simultanagnosia (Kim & Robertson, 2001). In this condition, when patients perceive an object they are unable to simultaneously perceive another object. Thus if a picture of a bus and a car is presented to the patient and they are asked to name the object present they may say "bus". If asked what the other

Figure 5.4 **A typical clock drawing by a patient with left neglect**
When asked to draw objects from memory, patients with left neglect typically miss off features from the left hand side. A very common observation
is that when asked to draw a clock only the right hand side is shown, with an
attempt to include all the numbers down this side.

object is, they may reply that there is no other object, or that they do
not know. It is as if, having lost spatial representation, they latch
onto an object and cling to this as an anchor in their visual field. Such a
view is supported by a recent study by Pavese, Coslett, Saffran, and
Buxbaum (2002). In this study, patients with simultanagnosia were
found to be able to name two objects in a display if they were alternated every 500 ms. The authors suggest, therefore, that the problem
is that the patients cannot disengage. Having perceived one object,
they cannot move from it to perceive a second object. Further work
will be required to explore the exact nature of this inability to disengage. Is it that the object somehow "holds" the person's attention,
like a magnet? Or is it that the person is reluctant to move away from
this visual reference point, having attained it? Thus it seems that the
occipital-parieto-frontal pathway processes space location, and this is
grossly disturbed in bilateral damage, leaving simultanagnosic patients
adrift in a visual sea with no compass, such that they grasp at any

visual landmark, which they are then reluctant to leave. In unilateral brain damage, this loss of the visual chart seems to affect only the contralesional side, leading the patient to attend only to the unaffected (ipsilesional) side.

Unilateral neglect does not only affect a patient's ability to perceive the external world, it also appears to affect internal representations. In a classic study, Bisiach and Luzzati (1978) asked patients to imagine themselves standing in the Plaza del Duomo in Milan. They were asked to imagine that they were standing at one end of the square, and to describe the scene as they could see it from their imagination. What they found was that patients with left neglect would give an accurate description of the right side of the square. The question is, had the patients lost the representation of the left side of the square, or were they simply "neglecting" it? In an ingenious manipulation, Bisiach and Luzzati asked the patients to imagine themselves walking across the square to the opposite side and turning to face the way they had come. Now they were looking backwards across the square, so that what was previously on the right was now on their left and vice versa. Once again they were asked to describe the square. As if by magic, what the patients had previously neglected to describe came into their imaginary view and they accurately described what was previously neglected, the former left side of the square as it now appeared on their right. What they had previously described only a minute before now mysteriously disappeared into the murky shadows of the patient's now neglected left side of the image.

The above study seems to present a convincing account that even internal representations are neglected in patients with the condition, and further that internal imagery may share the same substrate as external stimuli, i.e. that visual circuits serve both vision and imagery. A recent interesting study on this theme (Beschin, Cocchini, Della Sala, & Logie, 1997) suggested that in fact an internal representation can be neglected while outward perception is intact. In the study, a 67-year-old stroke victim neglected new and old visual imagery, but there was no perceptual or personal neglect. Neither of these studies explains how the neglect phenomenon comes about. The majority of such accounts put forward deficits in the processes of visual attention.

Humphreys and Riddoch (1992) suggested that neglect might be due to impaired orienting of attention. When we are asked to bisect a line, a common task given to neglect patients, normal individuals will scan along the length of the line to ensure that they are taking into account the whole of its length. Neglect patients fail to carry out this operation, instead assuming that the left-most edge of the line occurs at a point some way short of its actual end point in their neglected zone. Evidence for this comes from the fact that patients are able to use appropriate cues to improve their line bisection skills. For example Halligan, Manning, & Marshall (1991) showed that if patients were instructed to place their hand at the left-most edge of the stimuli, then their performance improved. They were able to use their left hand as a visual anchor, ensuring that they scanned the whole of the line. Thus according to Humphreys and Riddoch (1992), patients are able to make use of such cues and hence the problem is their inability to spontaneously make use of such strategies.

A similar account was put forward by Heilman and Valenstein (1979), who suggested that the right hemisphere might be responsible for orienting attention to both the left and right side of space, whereas the left hemisphere is responsible only for the right. Thus, in right neglect, due to a left hemisphere lesion, the deficit declines as the intact right hemisphere is able to compensate for the inability of the damaged left hemisphere to orient to the right. When the right hemisphere is damaged, however, orientation to the left is lost and the left hemisphere is unable to compensate. Similarly, Weintraub and Mesulam (1987) suggested that the right hemisphere may be responsible for attentional orientation to both the left and right visual fields.

Another suggestion is that neglect is caused by overly strong orienting to the ipsilesional side. For example, Ladavas (1990) showed that patients with neglect often show faster reaction times to stimuli presented on the right of the visual field than to stimuli presented in the centre. In a recent study, Sieroff and Urbanski (2002) found that when two stimuli are presented simultaneously to neglect patients, the left-most stimulus is likely to be ignored. This phenomenon is an example of extinction, whereby a stimulus on the left is ignored because a stimulus on the right appears to capture the whole of the patient's attention, thus supporting the view that there is some attentional bias to the right hand side in left neglect.

A further view is that patients are unable to disengage their attention from a stimulus. Having engaged a right-most stimulus, their attention is captured and they are not able to release their attentional focus and move it elsewhere. Such a view was put forward by Posner et al. (1984) and more recently by d'Erme, Robertson, Bartolomeo, and Daniele (1992). In the latter study, patients expected to see a target appear, on either the left or right side of a screen. In one condition the stimuli were presented on a blank screen, in another the spatial locations in which targets would appear was demarcated by two boxes. In the latter condition neglect was increased. This is explained by the fact that with the two boxes present there is always a cue to the right, which engages the patient's attention and makes it difficult to disengage and move their focus to the left.

Thus there are a number of views as to how neglect could arise from attentional deficits, due to ineffective orienting, a rightward bias, or an inability to disengage from a rightward stimulus. Humphreys and Riddoch (1992) attempt a synthesis of these accounts, which they referred to as an interacting attentional mechanisms account. In this view, a variety of attentional mechanisms are seen as operating in the brain, which together produce the phenomenon of unilateral neglect. The idea that several processes interact to form the phenomenon of neglect is an interesting and timely one, given that there are a number of competing proposals, each of which seems to have a measure of support.

Exactly why left neglect tends to remain a problem in patients is only partly addressed by these fairly static accounts. Recognizing this, Robertson (1993) attempted to account for the persistence of left compared to right neglect in patients. Robertson noticed that left neglect was often associated with a digit span discrepancy in his patients, such that their forward digit span was often significantly superior to their backwards digit span. Since backwards digit span is thought to rely far more on attentional mechanisms, as opposed to short-term memory capacity, Robertson hypothesized that the patients may have an attentional deficit, and that this might explain the persistence of the left neglect. He put forward the possible mechanism, explaining that patients with vigilance and arousal deficits may be less likely to pay attention to their neglect proneness, and therefore less likely to initiate strategies to cope with these deficits. Further studies have shown that deficits on a simple tone counting task, a measure of sustained attention from the Test of Everyday Attention (see Chapter 3), were associated with visual neglect (Robertson et al., 1997a). Also, sustained attention ability is closely linked to functional outcome following stroke (Robertson, Ridgeway, Greenfield, & Parr, 1997b), suggested that this skill underlies general coping responses and awareness of visual neglect. Finally, Robertson, Tegner, Tham, and Lo (1995) showed that attention training improved performance on measures of neglect, leaving control measures unimproved. The attention training involved a task quite dissimilar to the measures of neglect, so the authors cannot be accused of training to the outcome directly. The technique of using control measures to verify that improvement occurs only on specified target measures is a common one, and shows that the attention training produced specific improvements on the neglect tasks, rather than general improvements across the board.

Thus we have seen that the fairly common phenomenon of unilateral visual neglect, which produces striking behaviour in many patients following stroke, can be explained by a number of different attentional mechanisms. As Humphreys and Riddoch suggest (1993), the best view may be a synthesis, with deficits in a number of systems interacting to produce the condition. In lay terms, we can perhaps put ourselves in the shoes of the unfortunate stroke victims, who awake one morning in hospital to discover that they now have a whole host of difficulties on their left hand side, with weakness in their left arm and leg. As far as they know, their vision is unaffected but soon the nurses are remarking that they seem to be leaving all the food on the left side of their dinner plate. Whereas right neglect patients quickly come to appreciate the difficulty and find ways of overcoming it, left neglect patients are less aware, and in any case frequently feel tired and lethargic. This left side of space now has a vague and unappealing feel to it, leading patients to concentrate on the right hand side, and when given a focus on that side they choose to linger on that rather than force themselves to deal with the uncertainties of the left side. Over the months and years the difficulties linger as the patients fail to come to terms with the deficit. We are still some way off knowing how adequate an account this is but it is encouraging that significant strides are being made in terms of being able to help patients with this disabling and common condition (e.g. Robertson et al., 1995).

Summary

This chapter has shown how neurophysiological studies have pointed to certain parts of the brain being involved in selective attention, particularly the extrastriate visual cortex and the parietal lobes. Evidence of selective attention deficits was then discussed for two conditions in which such deficits have often been hypothesized, Alzheimer's disease and schizophrenia. Other conditions were then considered, including closed head injury and stroke. A phenomenon that occurs in the latter condition, unilateral neglect, was then considered in some depth. Different theoretical accounts of the phenomenon were discussed and it was suggested that the best eventual account may involve a synthesis of such views. Finally, a particular view of why left neglect persists was described, and it was shown how this has led to treatment approaches for this very disabling condition. In the final analysis, the worth of neuropsychology is more likely to be judged by the extent to which we are able to help patients lead a better quality of life rather than by our ability to construct ever more technical and finer-sounding theories that linger on the minutiae of mental life.

Controlling attention

Overview

THE HUMAN COGNITIVE system is dynamic, capable of constantly changing its focus in response to environmental contingencies, while at the same time allowing individuals to put in sustained effort to achieve some goal. Often the achievement of a larger goal will require several smaller goals to be satisfied on the way to the solution, and in many circumstances there may be considerable ambiguity about how a particular goal is to be achieved. In other words, we are able to solve quite difficult problems in our day-to-day lives and sometimes solving those problems requires considerable thought and ingenuity. At the same time we are able to monitor our performance and, if we decide that we are not making progress, we can switch to a different task or try another approach.

A number of tasks, which psychologists have either come across or devised, appear to tap into this aspect of our abilities. Such tasks typically require the solution of some abstract problem, with several steps to be satisfied along the way.

Neuropsychologists quickly discovered that head-injured patients have trouble with such tasks, and that these difficulties are associated with frontal lesions. Other tasks also seem to be sensitive to such lesions, e.g. the Stroop task. More recently, such tasks have come to be called tests of "executive" function, for example Baddeley and Hitch used the term to refer to the control processes in their model of working memory (Baddeley & Hitch, 1974). Typical findings in head injury on a number of such standard tasks will be outlined.

Given the frontal view of schizophrenia (dopamine systems implicated in the condition are frontally located; see Glossary), it is not surprising that researchers have explored the possibility of deficits in this area underlying the condition. A number of findings are reviewed.

It is suggested that executive deficits may be a previously neglected feature of dementia, including Alzheimer's disease and in particular frontotemporal dementia. Work from the last decade is described, along with some discussion of the notion that dual tasking is an executive ability.

Finally, the control of attention in children will be considered in relation to attention deficit hyperactivity disorder (ADHD). As will be seen, inhibition has traditionally been seen as the key deficit in this condition. More recently it has also been suggested that there might be more widespread executive impairments. An overarching theory of frontal dysfunction in ADHD will be considered and lessons drawn for how this work can help us to view attentional control functions in adults.

Introduction

A fundamental aspect of our experience as human beings is free will. At any given moment in time we have the impression that we are doing whatever it is we are doing because at that point in time we have chosen to do it. As you sit now, reading this book, you are doing so because at this point in time you have chosen to do this instead of any other activity (a very wise decision too, if I may say so!). In a moment, perhaps following this suggestion, you may decide to go to the kitchen and put on the kettle to make a cup of coffee. Again, this follows an active conscious decision to carry out some other activity for a time.

Theories of attention clearly have to allow for this aspect of our behaviour if they are to be comprehensive. For example, consider a Digit Span task (in which you have to keep a sequence of numbers in mind). This is a relatively simple task, and we can develop straightforward theories about how people carry it out. Let's try a short digit span sequence now. Read the following sequence of numbers, then close your eyes, wait for a few seconds, and then see if you can still say the words, without looking at the page again. Ready?

One, nine, three, seven, two, six, four.

Now, think for a moment about how you did that. Most people report that they say the numbers over to themselves, using some kind of inner voice. In fact most people report that their experience of thought is an inner voice that speaks out their thoughts as they go through life. If, while trying to do the task, you suddenly heard something interesting on the television in the background (if like me you have the bad habit of reading with the television on), then you may have chosen to stop rehearsing the numbers for a second and instead diverted your attention to the news story. It is this process, of deciding to switch your attention from one task to another, that we are trying to describe when we talk about attentional control.

According to Baddeley and Hitch's working memory model (1974), when we keep a set of numbers in mind, we rehearse them using a verbal process they called "the articulatory loop" (later renamed "the phonological loop"). Other processes, responsible for the moment-by-moment voluntary attentional control of the system were labelled "the central executive", the term reflecting their role in co-ordinating other cognitive processes. Shallice (1988) put forward a similar theory, also accounting for attentional control processes. This was termed the supervisory attentional system (see Chapter 1). In Shallice's account, much of our behaviour is governed by automatic conditioned responses to the environment. Most of the time, according to Shallice, we go through life on a sort of autopilot. As we walk into a room and decide to put the light on, our hand automatically reaches for the switch and performs the necessary action. It requires little conscious thought or effort. Occasionally, the operation of this autopilot can be seen through so-called "action-slips". For example, while thinking deeply about something in the kitchen, we might inadvertently put the milk in the oven, having meant to put it in the fridge. Or in an unfamiliar room we may find ourselves groping in the dark for the light switch before we realize this is not our room and the light switch is likely to be in a different place. When we need to deviate from these automated responses, the normal tendency has to be inhibited. Thus for Shallice, inhibition plays a key role in control of attention, a view which resonates with Barkley's (1997) recent theorizing about control in attention deficit disorder.

It has long been known that patients with damage to the frontal lobes can undergo changes to their personality and their ability to carry out activities of daily living (Schwartz, Mayer, Fitzpatrick-DeSalme, & Montgomery, 1993). It has also been established for some time that such patients show impaired performance on certain kinds of task. In particular, frontal lesions seem to give rise to difficulties in planning, concept production, maintaining a task schema, or inhibiting an automatic response (Levin, Fletcher, Kufera, & Harward,

1996). One theory of frontal lobe function (Fuster, 1989) suggests that the frontal lobes perform several key processes. The first, according to Fuster, is to inhibit behaviours and control interference. Inhibition means to delay or put off a behaviour that is normally elicited by a stimulus, and this function is required if we are going to learn new behaviours. So, if you are trying to learn a new language that involves different pronunciation rules to your own (e.g. the sounds made by certain letter combinations in Spanish differ from those in English), then you would have to inhibit the tendency to want to pronounce the words the way you would in your main language. Similarly, to perform a complex task may involve a considerable amount of thought, and carrying this out requires not being distracted. Thus if we are playing a difficult game of chess, we may have to concentrate hard on the next move, not allowing a nearby conversation to distract us (in fact some chess players become rapidly agitated if there is the slightest distraction while they are trying to play an important game). Besides inhibition and interference control, Fuster (1989) puts forward working memory functions. These are processes that allow behavioural sequences to be formulated over a period of time, e.g. planning a sequence of moves at chess. Time is a key issue here. Formulating complex behavioural responses may require the integration of information from past events together with current sensory input and envisaged sequences of events in the future. According to the theory, these two basic processes of inhibition/interference control and working memory are dissociable. The former is said to be located in the orbital frontal lobes along with their connections to the ventromedial area of the striatum (Iverson & Dunnett, 1990) and the latter in the dorsolateral area of the prefrontal cortex. There is now considerable evidence supporting these kinds of dissociation and localization of these different aspects of functioning (D'Esposito et al., 1995; Goldman-Rakic, 1995; Knights, Grabowecky, & Scabini, 1995; Milner, 1995; Rypma, Berger, & D'Esposito, 2002; Thompson-Schill et al., 2002; Vendrell et al., 1995; Williams & Goldman-Rakic, 1995).

It is probably useful in exploring the issue of control to consider further the types of task that have been used to assess frontal lobe functioning. Bearing in mind Fuster's (1989) view of frontal lobe functions, we would expect such tasks to fall into two broad camps, those that primarily assess the inhibition/interference element and those that primarily tap the working memory/temporal integration element, with some tasks tapping both.

Taking the first dimension of inhibition/interference control, probably the best known and certainly very widely used measure is the Stroop task, Stroop (1935). Reading is highly automated in adult readers, and this causes difficulty on the Stroop, where colour names have to be ignored in preference to the actual colour of the font being used, e.g. shouting out "blue" to the word "red" written in blue ink. Patients with frontal lesions have been found to be impaired on the task (Holst & Vilkki, 1988). From observing patient behaviour it seems as if they are unable to maintain the inhibitory task goal in mind, and consequently frequently revert to reading the words, having to be reminded that they should be saying the colour.

In terms of the working memory dimension, probably the most widely used has been the Wisconsin Card Sorting task (WCST). In this task the person being examined is shown a set of four stimulus cards, each depicting a series of shapes that differ in number, shape, and colour. As described in Chapter 3, the testee has to work out which rule the examiner is thinking of by sorting the cards, and find new rules as they change. The task clearly involves considerable temporal integration, remembering the previous move, and planning the next. One could also argue that an element of inhibition is involved, since when the rule changes one has to inhibit the previous rule and respond with a new one.

Another popular task is known as the Tower of Hanoi and its derivatives (see Figure 1.10). The task involves moving a set of discs from the left to right peg, following a set of rules. The task seems to draw heavily on the working memory component of Fuster's (1989) model.

More recently, the Six Elements task has been found to be useful (Wilson, Evans, Emslie, Alderman, & Burgess, 1998). As described in Chapter 3, the testee has to work through a sequence of six subtasks, without spending too much time on any one in particular. This test was found in a battery of frontal tasks to be the most consistent in identifying frontal lesions, and problems in performing the task have been linked to the concept of "goal neglect" (Duncan, et al., 1996;

Duncan, Johnson, Swales, & Freer, 1997). Goal neglect is the suggestion that patients with frontal lesions fail to carry out certain kinds of task well because they fail to monitor the task requirements and therefore leave important aspects of the problem incomplete. Like the Wisconsin Card Sorting task, one might also argue that a strong element of inhibition is required for the Six Elements task since, to perform well, one has to inhibit performance on one of the tasks in order to move in a timely manner onto one of the other tasks. One can imagine that patients with inhibition difficulties might experience considerable problems in moving from one element to the other.

Thus a range of tasks have been put forward that are said to be able to detect frontal lobe dysfunction. If we had to try and spot a common link between them, we might say that they all involve intense mental concentration and a degree of novelty. As Fuster (1989) noted, many of the tasks involve a degree of temporal integration, while others involve inhibition. As stated earlier, these two dimensions receive considerable support from scanning studies in terms of localization of the two functions in different parts of the frontal lobes. Experimental support for this comes from a study using factor analysis.

Burgess, Alderman, Evans, Emslie, and Wilson (1998) indicated that a wide range of frontal-type tasks seemed to measure inhibition, intentionality, and what they termed executive memory. This seems to fit to some degree with Fuster's view. Furthermore, Duncan et al. (1997) pointed out that different frontal tasks probably do not depend on the same processes, since the correlations between performance on the different tasks are low, again in accord with Fuster's notion that the frontal lobes perform a variety of functions. It has been noted that the various frontal tasks do not invariably identify all frontal cases (Baddeley, Della Sala, Papagno, & Spinnler, 1997). It remains to be seen whether the most sensitive tasks are those that load heavily on Fuster's two factors. There is some support for this thought. For example, in the Baddeley et al. (1997) study, word fluency was far more sensitive than the Wisconsin Card Sorting task (i.e. it was better able to detect which patients had frontal lesions). Word fluency requires participants to generate as many words beginning with a particular letter as they can in 1 minute; the letter is typically F (followed by A and S). The task requires a heavy degree of temporal monitoring and integration, since successful subjects will monitor their progress carefully as they proceed and implement a variety of retrieval strategies. At the same time there is a strong tendency to repeat words and break the rules (no names or plurals), and these tendencies need to be inhibited. Frontal patients typically say the same word over many times, give proper names, and generate derivatives and plurals (e.g. they might say "film, film, films, filmed, Fred, far, Frederick . . ., etc.). Thus it seems that word fluency incorporates a number of the elements envisaged by Fuster (1989).

Executive processes, then, seem to measure our ability to direct our free will. This means being able to concentrate processing resources on the resolution of complex novel tasks, while inhibiting irrelevant responses and staying free from distraction. Thus the frontal lobes (which after all represent a large proportion of the human brain) probably serve a number of separate and discrete processes. Exactly how many processes there are, and to what degree they overlap or are independent, remains to be determined, but at least we have made a start in delineating these processes and even localizing them to different regions.

In recent years it has become quite common to associate these frontal tasks with the notion of executive processing (see Stuss and Gow [1992] for a review of the issue), and the term "dysexecutive" has become frequent in the literature to denote patients with frontal lobe lesions who are experiencing problems with their planning and control processes and experiencing problems in their daily lives.

We will now review evidence for frontal deficits in three important conditions: head injury, schizophrenia, and dementia. Finally, we will look at the only condition considered in this book which is specific to children, attention deficit hyperactivity disorder.

Control and head injury

As mentioned earlier, it has long been appreciated that patients with head injury have problems in performing certain kinds of tasks if there are lesions in the frontal areas. A classic example of this can be found back at the dawn of neuropsychology, in the case of Phineas Gage, one of the earliest neuropsychological case studies. Phineas Gage was a railway worker, engaged in the hazardous occupation of rock blasting, which was done to clear new cuttings through rock formations. The technique involved boring a long, thin hole into the rock, which was then packed with gun powder and ignited with a fuse. Packing the gun powder involved ramming it into the hole with a metal rod. Unfortunately for Phineas Gage, one day while performing this dangerous activity the gun powder ignited, blasting the metal rod into the air like an elongated bullet. It passed into Phineas Gage's lower jaw, through the frontal part of his head and out of the top left fontal part of his skull. Miraculously, Gage survived this shocking trauma, and went on to live for many years. The behavioural changes that took place as a result of this accident were well documented by medics at the time. In particular, he was noted to become child like in his behaviour, disinhibited, soon to anger, and needing assistance in organizing his affairs (Macmillan, 2000).

Since Gage, researchers have made considerable progress in understanding the processes served by the frontal lobes. Patients have been found to be impaired on a number of types of specific tasks. Probably the most well known of these is the Wisconsin Card Sorting task (e.g. Flashman, Horner, & Freides [1991]; see Demakis [2003] for a meta-analytical review of sensitivity to frontal damage). Basically, as previously described, patients have to sort cards according to a rule that they have to discover; from time to time the rule is changed, requiring patients to work out the new rule. Frontal patients typically have considerable difficulty with this, often committing large numbers of preservative errors. In other words, even though patients have been told that a particular rule is now incorrect, they continue to use it, despite receiving negative feedback over and over again. The current author has frequently observed patients who, having established an initial rule, continue to use that rule until all the rest of the pack of cards has been exhausted (this can involve being told a rule is incorrect 42 times on the modified Wisconsin Card Sorting task!). It seems as if, having latched onto a rule, the patient is somehow completely unable to envisage any other possible rule (in fact, a similar phenomenon occurs in some normal subjects who, having discovered two of the possible three rules, become somehow blinded to the possibility of the third). Another way of viewing this would be to suggest that the patient is unable to inhibit the existing rule and move on to the next. In fact most complex "frontal" tasks could be impaired for a variety of reasons, and it is perfectly possible that patients could have difficulties on a task for a variety of reasons, each of which could be described as frontal. For example, one patient may have trouble keeping in mind his or her sequence of responses, while another might not be able to inhibit a previous response.

Patients with frontal lesions are frequently impaired on tasks that require planning a sequence of moves. One such task is the Tower of Hanoi and its derivatives, e.g. the Tower of London (Shallice, 1982, 1988; see Figure 1.10). As with the Wisconsin Card Sorting task, patients seem to be unable to adequately monitor their performance. Their sequence of moves is poorly thought out and they make many perseverative responses, i.e. repeating a sequence of unproductive moves several times.

Frontal lesions also often produce deficits in patients ability to inhibit a pre-potent response, the best example being on the Stroop task. As previously mentioned, on this task patients have to try and ignore colour words while trying to name the font colour of the stimulus, e.g. the word "red" written in blue. Patients with frontal lesions find this very hard (Holst & Vilkki, 1988), typically trying to read the stimulus words and having to be constantly reminded that they need to identify the font colour. The current author has frequently had to resort to covering the word and just leaving the last letter exposed to get such patients back on track. With just the last letter exposed the patient can be asked to name its colour, and once again grasps the instructions for a time. It is as if the patient is unable to inhibit the powerful automatic response, despite knowing what it is he or she is required to do.

As described above, frontal patients frequently have difficulty inhibiting an automated response, as seen on the Stroop task. Similarly, if they are currently responding in a certain way on a task and are suddenly required to change the type of response, this can cause difficulties. Rieger, Gauggel, and Burmeister (2003) presented patients with a two-choice reaction time task, in which on some trials a tone indicated that the patient was to withhold a response. The frontal patients were significantly impaired compared to orthopaedic controls.

Tasks requiring spontaneous strategy generation and performance monitoring also cause considerable difficulties. Word fluency tasks are a good example of this (see the preceding discussion of Baddeley et al.'s (1997) paper using the F, A, S task). On such tasks, frontal patients tend to produce words at random and frequently repeat words they have said already (perseveration) (Holst & Vilkki, 1988).

More recently, the constellation of functions served by the frontal lobes has been expanded. For example, the co-ordination of several simultaneous tasks, as required during dual task procedures, is now frequently ascribed to the frontal lobes (e.g. Allain, Etcharry-Bouyx, & Le Gall, 2001; Baddeley et al., 1997). Baddeley et al. (1997) in fact found dual tasking to be more sensitive to frontal lobe dysfunction than traditional "frontal" measures. They also found that dual task impairment was a reliable indicator of which patients had behavioural dysfunction in their everyday lives, but were unable to suggest why this might be the case. It may be that Fuster's inhibition/distraction process is heavily implicated in dual tasking, since lack of inhibition is often suggested to underlie the behavioural problems experienced by frontal patients (e.g. impulsivity, aggression). Interestingly, Alderman (1996) pointed out that patients who were unable to benefit from a rehabilitation programme then depended on behavioural methods were likely to have dual tasking difficulties. This leads to the very tentative suggestion that the ability to benefit from a very behaviouristic rehabilitation programme is dependent on intact executive processes, as indexed by the dual task performance.

Recently, attention has also turned to the role of executive processes in task switching. An example of such a task would be to be given a list of numbers and asked to alternately indicate whether the number is odd/even or bigger/smaller than 5. In such a situation some effort is required to keep track of which categorization you are currently on. Mecklinger, von Cramon, Springer, and Matthes von Cramon (1999) found brain-damaged patients to be impaired on the task, but more so if there was damage to the left hemisphere, indicating a likelihood of language deficits. This fits in with another recent study (Baddeley, Baddeley, Bucks, & Wilcock, 2001), which found that task switching was impaired by concurrent articulation. It seems that Vygotsky (1962, 1978, 1987) may be making a comeback into modern cognitive psychology, with the notion that language has an important role to play in controlling and guiding behaviour (this view has also been put forward in strong terms by Barkley [1997], who relies heavily on Bronowski [1977] and the notion of internalized speech in his executive theory of ADHD; see later).

Looking back at the range of tasks on which performance has been found to be impaired following frontal lobe damage, it can be seen that they are quite varied. Word fluency, for example, seems to have little in common with the Tower of Hanoi task. The question then arises as to whether these tasks, despite their surface dis-similarities, actually tap into some core skill common to them all and mediated via the frontal lobes. Alternatively, it might be that the frontal lobes serve many separate functions. What therefore links these varied tasks together is simply the fact that the myriad processes they assess are all located in adjacent parts of the brain. At this point in time it is hard to distinguish these two possibilities and there is some empirical support for both suggestions. For example, Spikman, Deelman, and van Zomeren (2000) suggested that the main finding that differentiated their group of frontal patients from other patients and controls was their ability to perform a route-finding task. This, they suggest, indicates that the key deficit is in the inability to use internal cues and a reliance on external cues, i.e. a monitoring deficit. Certainly, looking at the range of tasks above, they all seem to require careful internal monitoring of performance. On the other hand, Duncan et al. (1997) suggested that a range of frontal-type tasks failed to show much relationship with one another, i.e. failing the Wisconsin Card Sorting task does not necessarily imply poor word fluency per-formance. Of all the tasks used in their study, Duncan et al. suggested the Six Elements task was the best in terms of sensitivity to frontal lobe dysfunction. Theoretically, Duncan et al. refer to the concept of "goal neglect" to explain impaired performance on frontal tasks, in other words patients fail to keep goals in mind and monitor their progress towards them. So on the one hand these authors draw attention to the lack of similarity between frontal-type tasks but at the same time wish to propose a core deficit for frontal patients in terms of goal neglect. Then we have Fuster's (1989) view that there are two core frontal functions, inhibition and working memory (the latter sounding very similar to Duncan et al.'s notion of goal neglect). In a sense, Fuster's view seems to be a halfway-house between the two extremes of a core executive process underlying all executive tasks and many separate processes specific to certain tasks. (This sounds rather like the debate that has taken place for many years in the area of intelligence research. Is there a single underlying ability that explains performance on all IQ tests [g], or are there lots of specific abilities underlying performance on each different type of task? Perhaps the similarity should not be too surprising. Duncan, Burgess, and Emslie [1995] recently suggested that Cattell's fluid intelligence test was an excellent "frontal" task. A later paper (Duncan et al., 2000), based on imaging, went on to suggest that the frontal lobes may even be the seat of "g" [and thus we finally have an answer to that old favourite of individual differences examiners "what do intelligence tests measure?"]).

In fact, it is possible and indeed probable that both accounts are correct. There may well be overarching control functions served by the frontal lobes, and at the same time more specific control processes located in more discrete structures.

Whatever theoretical direction accounts of executive function may take, it is clear that these processes are important to the day-to-day functioning of patients. Schwartz et al. (1993) pointed out that patients with frontal lesions often have great difficulty in carrying out the normal range of daily activities. In a similar vein, Pollens, McBratnie, and Burton (1988) suggested that executive functions may be important in allowing patients to benefit from rehabilitation. Thus while patients may perform well on many traditional tasks of intellectual function, if they have frontal lesions they may be disorganized and unable to benefit from environmental cues, becoming lost in situations where there is a lack of external cues to guide their behaviour.

Despite the lack of clarity with respect to the precise nature of "frontal lobe" or "executive" functions, some workers have recently sought to develop comprehensive batteries of executive function. The

Behavioural Assessment of the Dysexecutive Syndrome (Wilson et al., 1998, described in Norris and Tate, 2000), besides offering a range of tests, also sets out to have some degree of ecological validity. Given the lack of theoretical clarity over executive function, it is not clear what empirically derived guidelines these authors followed in the choice of tests, other than that they should require a degree of internal monitoring and strategizing, and have good face validity as measures of frontal lobe function. Nevertheless, the battery is a welcome addition to the range of tests available to clinicians for the assessment of this important area, and is becoming deservedly popular. In particular, the battery includes a version of the Six Elements task, praised by Duncan et al. (1997) as the most sensitive of a range of so-called "frontal" measures. More recently, an ecologically valid test similar to the Six Elements task has been presented (Alderman, Burgess, Knight, & Henman, 2003).

Control deficits in schizophrenia

The treatment of schizophrenia changed dramatically in the 1950s with the advent of phenothiazine medication. Drugs such as chlorpromazine for the first time seemed to be able to directly reduce psychotic behaviour. As a result, the number of long-stay beds required for schizophrenic patients has been hugely reduced. Most patients nowadays are treated with short stays on psychiatric units in general hospitals, rather than spending many months or years in long-stay asylums as might have happened in the past.

Investigation of these medications has revealed that they influence the dopamine systems located in the frontal regions of the brain. Given this, much interest has focused upon the possibility that schizophrenia results from frontal pathology. If frontal dopamine systems are over active in schizophrenia (there is converging evidence of this from amphetamine-induced psychosis and occasional psychotic features in some patients being treated with L-dopa for Parkinson's disease) then it may be possible to spot deficits in performance of schizophrenic patients on frontal-type tasks. Furthermore, given the possibility that schizophrenia may to some degree be genetically linked, it is possible that deficits on such tests might act as some kind of marker of vulnerability. Thus much effort has gone into assessing schizophrenic patients, their relatives, and others said to have schizophrenic features in their personality and behaviour (so called schizotypy). Given that neuropsychologists have been successful in identifying a number of tasks that appear to be able to detect frontal lobe damage in head-injured patients as described above, it is not surprising that researchers have taken these tests and applied them in schizophrenia research. It has to be said, however, that this research has frequently not been well informed. Researchers in the area frequently seem to be confused about the conceptualization of some well-known tasks. For example, the Stroop task is sometimes described as a test of divided attention or a test of general attention, rather than a test of inhibition.

A number of studies have tested a cohort of schizophrenic patients on a battery of frontal tests and report deficits in at least some of them (Evans, Chua, McKenna, & Wilson, 1997; Ihara, Berrios, & McKenna, 2000; Marczewski, van der Linden, & Laroi, 2001; McGrath, Scheldt, Hengstsberger, & Dark, 1997). Specific deficits have been reported on the WCST (Bustini, et al., 1999; Goldman, Axelrod, Tandon, & Berent, 1991; McGrath et al., 1997; Saoud et al., 2000; Stratta et al., 1997). McGrath et al. (1997) and Brebion et al. (1996) reported deficits amongst patients on the Stroop task, although Taylor, Kornblum, and Tandon (1996) failed to find such a result. Planning was found to be impaired by Pantelis et al. (1997), Morice and Delharty (1996) and Hutton et al. (1998). Recently, Giovannetti, Goldstein, Schullery, Barr, and Bilder (2003) found that first-episode schizophrenic patients generated fewer words in a semantic fluency task and made more perseverative errors than controls. On the same theme, Kremen, Seidman, Faraone, and Tsuang (2003) reported impaired phonemic (ability to generate words to a letter, e.g. F) and semantic (ability to generate names of animals) fluency in schizophrenic patients. The phonemic impairment, they suggest, represents impaired executive processes (while semantic fluency impairment represents abnormal semantic organization).

A number of studies have found impairments on frontal-type tasks in people said to be at risk for schizophrenia. These include

Suhr (1997), Poreh, Ross, and Whitman (1995), Saoud et al. (2000), and Cosway et al. (2000). The study by Poreh and colleagues pointed out that the "executive" deficit was specific, i.e. other aspects of cognition such as memory and learning were intact. However, Stratta et al. (1997) reported no frontal deficits in their at-risk sample.

From the studies that have been summarized so far, it certainly does seem as if the balance of evidence is in favour of the notion of frontal deficits in schizophrenia. However, there are a number of issues to complicate such a straightforward view. The first is to do with positive and negative symptoms. Schizophrenic symptoms are often categorized under two headings. Positive symptoms are the more active, psychotic behaviours, e.g. auditory hallucinations, paranoia. Negative symptoms are absence behaviours, e.g. lack of motivation, apathy. A number of studies have suggested that frontal deficits may be restricted to those patients with predominantly negative symptoms (Bryson, Whelahan, & Bell, 2001; Buchanan, Strauss, Kirkpatrick, & Holstein, 1994; Hill, Gur, & Gur, 2001).

A final complication to the frontal view of schizophrenia is that such deficits might reflect a general intellectual decline instead of a specific frontal deficit. Studies putting forward such a view include Kenny et al. (1997), Hill et al. (2001), Bilder et al. (2000), Laws, McKenna, and McCarthy (1999) and Poole Ober, Shenaut, and Vinogradov (1999). These studies point out that other aspects of cognition are often impaired, e.g. memory, and that frontal deficits tend to be less evident in brighter patients. Such patients will tend to score higher on traditional ability tests, e.g. the Ravens Matrices, said to measure fluid intelligence. This latter construct involves the ability to reason and solve problems, and tests designed to assess it frequently look like classic "frontal" tasks. This view is further complicated by recent suggestions from Duncan and colleagues (e.g. 1997) that tests of frontal lobe functioning may in fact be tapping into fluid intelligence. Thus less intelligent participants are likely to exhibit the phenomena of goal neglect. In addition, Duncan found that tests of fluid intelligence (e.g. Cattell's test) perform well as measures of frontal lobe functioning, identifying frontal lobe damaged patients as well as traditional tests. In effect, Duncan et al. have pointed out that such patients may suffer a considerable decrease in their fluid intelligence. (Exactly why Cattell's fluid intelligence tests work well as an index of frontal lobe functioning has yet to be determined. It may be that the problems are highly original, and require considerable mental agility in their solution, i.e. the ability to generate a large number of candidate solutions. Since there are many problems, each of which has a very different solution, mental flexibility is required to switch rapidly from one problem to another. Finally, the problems are often made up of familiar-looking items, e.g. shapes, but whose salient characteristics subsequently turn out to be misleading, thus requiring inhibition of the obvious characteristics, e.g. a problem with familiar shapes where orientation turns out to be the critical feature.) If frontal lobe functioning is an aspect of fluid intelligence, then it is not surprising that highly intelligent schizophrenic patients are preserved on tests of this function, but this does not mean to say that such patients are performing at a level consistent with their other abilities. Answering this question requires an analysis that compares a patient's fluid abilities with his or her abilities on other tasks testing other functions, e.g. verbal knowledge. This latter variable is often taken as a good indicator of premorbid functioning. Furthermore, if, as intelligence theorists believe, fluid intelligence and its closely related concept of general intelligence, or g, are central to overall intelligence, then it is also possible that schizophrenic patients who suffer a decline in this area will suffer declines in other areas of functioning that are underpinned by it. Such other areas likely to be affected include memory and learning, whereas vocabulary might be less vulnerable. Laws et al.'s (1999) finding that performance in other areas of intellectual functioning is in fact considerably worse than frontal functioning is, however, not easily dismissed by these types of argument. Therefore frontal lobe deficits may not be the most prominent ones in schizophrenia, and are unlikely to be the root issue underlying the illness, according to these authors.

To summarize, it seems that performance on tests that have traditionally been thought to reflect frontal lobe functioning is impaired in many schizophrenic patients. It has been suggested that such deficits are more associated with the negative vegetative symptoms than with the positive. Given that many such tasks involve speeded responses, some of this could be due to generalized slowing in the condition (see

Chapter 4 for a discussion of the idea that executive deficits in head injury might be due to a slower speed of processing). Such deficits are less evident in more able patients, but this could be due to their starting with a greater level of processing resources at the onset of the condition. Some people with schizotypy also seem to have difficulties with these kinds of task. It seems to the current author that frontal lobe deficits may well be a feature of the condition, but they are not a core deficit. In other words, mental slowing and confusion will certainly impair one's ability to think clearly on mental reasoning tasks, but that inability is not what originates the early florid experience of schizophrenia, with its crushing paranoia, vivid auditory hallucinations, and unshakable delusions. In this view, mental confusion is the chicken of the psychotic egg. It should also be borne in mind that schizophrenia is far from a unitary disorder. Not all patients experience auditory hallucinations, for others paranoia is the main feature. Thus there is a need to consider the issue in terms of how frontal lobe processing is involved in the different subtypes of the condition.

Control and dementia

"Dementia" is a general term that simply means a global deterioration in intellectual functioning. The term does not imply anything about aetiology. Thus someone suffering from cognitive deficits as a result of very severe depression could be described as suffering from the "dementia syndrome of depression". Of the various causes of cognitive decline in the elderly, Alzheimer's disease is most common, accounting for over 50% of cases. This condition has a distinctive pathology, with large numbers of neurofibrillary tangles and amyloid plaques being found in the brain tissue (such pathology is evident to some extent in the brains of elderly people not diagnosed as suffering from dementia, which at one time led to the view that Alzheimer's disease is an exaggeration of the normal ageing process).

In the not too distant past (i.e. prior to the 1990s) Alzheimer's disease was seen primarily as a disorder of memory. This almost certainly reflects the fact that this aspect of the condition is frequently the most salient presenting feature in the clinic. Relatives often complain that the patient no longer recognizes them, or goes out shopping and gets lost, or puts things around the house and forgets where they are. Sometimes these symptoms become very pronounced and troublesome (which is often when relatives decide to seek help). For example, patients may lock family members out of the house because they are no longer certain who they are, or become violent and aggressive because they believe that someone has taken their things (the current author recalls the case of a patient who frequently phoned the police to complain that his van had been stolen, when in fact it had been sold 10 years before).

Thus the emphasis in the clinic when dealing with patients with possible Alzheimer's disease was on memory. Little attention was paid to other aspects of cognition. In fact, in the interests of not upsetting patients unnecessarily, many "dementia clinics" were renamed as "memory clinics" (perhaps in future they will be cognitive clinics).

In the 1990s it came to be recognized that patients with Alzheimer's disease also have other cognitive deficits, and indeed these other deficits might contribute to the memory problems. Thus Greene, Hodges, and Baddeley (1995) found that aspects of autobiographical memory were, as expected, impaired in patients with Alzheimer's disease. However, deficits in aspects of executive function, such as dual tasking and word fluency, were strongly associated with certain aspects of the autobiographical memory deficit. Thus the authors concluded that the memory deficits are due first to the loss of the memories themselves and, second, to the damage to executive retrieval processes. Thus patients with Alzheimer's disease can be seen as on the one hand loosing aspects of their memory and, on the other hand, being unable to retrieve what memories they have left.

Other aspects of executive function found to be impaired in these patients include random number generation (Brugger, Monsch, Salmon, & Butters, 1996), planning on the Porteus Maze task (Mack & Patterson, 1995), Stroop interference performance and cognitive estimates (Nathan, Wilkinson, Stammers, & Low, 2001), clock drawing (Royall, Cordes, & Polk 1998), and dual tasking (Baddeley et al., 2001). More will be said about dual tasking shortly.

Thus deficits on executive tasks can certainly form part of the picture in Alzheimer's disease. However, it is not always the case that such patients will have such deficits as prominent features, but where they do occur early in the disease then progression may be more rapid (Patterson, Mack, Geldmacher, & Whitehouse, 1996). Executive function deficits have also been implicated in the agitation and disinhibited behaviour that often occurs in the disease (Chen, Sultzer, Hinkin, Mahler, & Cummings, 1998). The authors suggest therefore that the neural substrate underlying such problem behaviours may well be located in the frontal regions. This would not be surprising, given that such behaviours are frequently observed in head-injured patients with frontal lesions (and Baddeley et al. [1997] found a link between behavioural difficulties and dual task performance). Such an insight could be an important one for future work, given that such behaviours are frequently cited by relatives as the problem leading to the final breakdown of the home care situation and thus to institutionalization.

It was stated previously that the ability to perform two tasks together, i.e. to dual task, has been put forward as an executive deficit in patients with Alzheimer's disease. One such prominent study was that of Baddeley et al. (2001). In fact, Baddeley et al. tested their patients on tasks of focused (simple and choice reaction time) and selective (visual search) attention as well. They suggested that if the attention deficit is a unitary phenomenon, perhaps due to loss of processing capacity, then performance on all the tasks should be uniformly impaired. What they found was that focused attention was relatively spared, selective attention was moderately impaired, while divided attention in a dual task paradigm was grossly impaired. Thus the attention deficit seen in Alzheimer's disease is not a unitary phenomenon, e.g. as might be caused by slowing in the speed of processing. The alternative might be that some brain areas, serving specific attentional functions, are more susceptible to damage or degradation in performance than other areas. The frontal areas, with widespread and diffuse connections to other brain regions, could be especially vulnerable to widespread diffuse cortical lesions, leading to the gross impairment of some executive functions but leaving other aspects of attention relatively intact.

However, not all studies are in accord with Baddeley et al. (2001). Perry, Watson, and Hodges (2000) found that sustained and divided attention was intact in their very mild cases, with only deficits in selective attention (in response inhibition and switching). Mild cases (as opposed to very mild cases) were impaired on all three aspects of attention. This is in accord with Baddeley et al., in that the slightly more advanced cases (Mini-mental State Examination (MMSE) of 16–23) did have divided attention deficits, but the differential pattern of deficits across the three domains was not seen (but then the design of this study did not set out with this objective in mind, whereas Baddeley et al. manipulated task difficulty in order to get at the issue of relative sparing). A further study supporting dual task deficits in such patients comes from Camicioli, Howieson, Lehman, and Kaye (1997). In this study, the walking performance of patients was impaired when they had to simultaneously perform a verbal fluency task. By contrast, Collette, van der Linden, Bechet, Belleville, and Salmon (1998) found that while their patients with Alzheimer's disease could not perform an executive span task, they could perform a dual task. The span task required the patients to reorder into alphabetical sequence a list of presented words (e.g. fish, cat, bird, dog, ant); the dual task was a combination of digit repetition and a visuomotor task.

At the present time, therefore, it remains uncertain whether there is a dual task deficit early in the course of Alzheimer's disease. Collete et al.'s (1998) study used a relatively small number of patients, with only 11 in the patient and control groups, which may have limited the power. At the same time, their dual task is a combination of two relatively straightforward tasks, and the results might have been different if the tasks had been more demanding. However, there is a methodological problem with some of the positive findings too. Camicioli et al. (1997), for example, combined the fairly straightforward task of walking with the acknowledged executive task of verbal fluency. If there is an executive deficit in the condition, then it should not be surprising that combining an executive task with a second task produces decrements on the latter (it's a bit like asking a one-legged man to ride a bicycle and recite Shakespeare). We can only fairly say that a dual task deficit exists, i.e. there is an impairment in the ability to handle two simultaneous tasks, where the two tasks being combined do not individually make heavy demands on the executive system. Ideally, performance on the individual tasks should be normal, with impairment only evident when the two are combined. Baddeley et al.'s study meets these criteria. Finally, it is possible that studies in the area are further confounded by the way different centres delineate different types of dementia. Alzheimer's disease, being the biggest category of dementia in older people, is still the most likely diagnosis to be applied to a patient in most centres. If there are then other features that suggest a refinement to this, some other label may be applied. For example, if attention appears to fluctuate and there are hallucinations, then Lewy body dementia may be suggested. If there are prominent frontal features, and if the centre is sensitive to the possibilities of frontal impairment, then a label of frontotemporal dementia might be applied. It is possible, therefore, that in some studies, the samples of patients with Alzheimer's disease include cases that in other centres would be differentiated as frontotemporal dementia. Thus studies would differ in the extent to which they find executive deficits in Alzheimer's disease. Centres that routinely differentiate frontotemporal dementia and exclude such cases from Alzheimer studies would be less likely to find executive deficits in the patients who remain.

If executive deficits are not necessarily core deficits in Alzheimer's disease, they most certainly are for so-called "frontotemporal" or "frontal variant frontotemporal" dementia (Duke & Kaszniack, 2000). Like Lewy body dementia (see Chapter 5 for details on this diagnosis), this condition has come to prominence in the last decade or so and in past times such patients most likely would simply have been described as "Alzheimer's" (and often probably still are). One of the major criteria used for distinguishing frontal variant dementia is the existence of executive deficits as shown by performance on frontal tasks. Recent studies in the literature claim to meet this criteria if performance is impaired on several such tasks, e.g. Trails version B and the Stroop. Lough, Gregory, and Hodges (2001) presumably defined their sample of frontal variant patients some other way, since they were described as having intact performance on executive tasks but an inability to perform "theory of mind" problems. Theory of mind problems require the testees to be able to put themselves into another person's shoes in order to arrive at a solution. A problem of this type was outlined in Chapter 2, in relation to Gregory et al.'s (2002) study. A scenario is given in which events happen to one character, which a second character remains unaware of. The problem requires the testee to take into account the fact that the second character is unaware of some of the events. The fact that in Lough et al.'s study the patients had trouble with such scenarios while being able to perform other executive tasks suggests that theory of mind may be an independent ability, distinct from other aspects of executive function (see the discussion above, that executive processes may be highly discrete and associate in some patients simply by virtue of being located in adjacent parts of the frontal lobes, as opposed to the view that such processes share some fundamental core process).

Deficits in executive function are also evident in other types of dementia. Litvan, Mohr, Williams, and Gomez (1991) found that their sample of patients with Parkinson's disease were more impaired on tasks of executive function than a group of Alzheimer's patients matched for overall severity of dementia. Similarly, Kramer, Reed, Mungas, Weiner, and Chui (2002) found executive deficits to be a prominent feature of subcortical ischaemic vascular disease.

Attention and control in children

Attention deficit hyperactivity disorder (ADHD) is a condition that is typically diagnosed in childhood, although it can exist unrecognized into adulthood. It frequently persists into adolescence and adulthood in those diagnosed. It is thought to affect somewhere between 5 and 10% of children, with the numbers increasing in recent years. Whether this is because the condition is becoming more frequent or is simply being recognized more is unclear.

Most teachers are nowadays familiar with the term ADHD, and can describe its typical presentation based upon children they have taught. Given the prevalence, there is typically at least one child thought to be affected in most primary classrooms. Current diagnostic schemes currently rely heavily on teacher impressions and ratings. Children with ADHD are difficult to settle. They seem to find it hard to stay on task for any length of time. Given an activity, they will be found wandering around the classroom, or being disruptive while

ATTENTION

the other children get on with their work. These children tend to be distractible and their concentration is easily broken by events going on around them. Another child going to the teacher for help will easily divert them from their own chore. At the same time, such children are less open to the kinds of controls and balances that can be used with other children. The promise of a future rewarding activity on completion of another more laborious task holds little sway with them. They live for the here and now.

The actual picture is a little more complicated than that which has been painted above. ADHD is currently broken down into two main types (Barkley, 1997). One is termed the "inattentive" type. In these children, the primary feature is an inability to concentrate over a period of time. The other type is often called "combined", indicating a mixture of inattentive features coupled with a tendency towards hyperactivity. Only the latter fully lives up to the term ADHD, and it has been suggested that the two types may in fact represent different disorders. For example, Dinn, Robbins, and Harris (2001) suggest that the two types may have different neuropsychological profiles, based upon different underlying pathology—orbitofrontal in the one case and dorsolateral prefrontal in the other. (Hale, Hariri, and McCracken [2000], in reviewing a series of scanning studies further support the role of frontal striatum in ADHD.) Similarly, Lockwood, Marcotte, and Stern (2001) suggested that executive deficits are found only in the combined type, and Houghton et al. (1999) found perseveration and response inhibition deficits only in the combined type. Thus there are different subtypes of ADHD, with different behavioural consequences, and much of what follows on executive deficits may primarily apply to the combined type.

Sustained attention and inhibition

A common finding reflected in much of the literature is that ADHD children have particular difficulty with tests of sustained attention (Barkley, Edwards, Laneri, Fletcher, & Metevia; 2001; Gansler et al., 1998; Manly et al., 2001; Okazaki, Kawakubo, Hosokawa, & Maekawa, 2001; Perugini et al., 2000). Typically in these studies a form of continuous performance task is used, in which the child has to monitor closely an ongoing stimulus and respond to certain targets. For example, a letter may be displayed in the centre of a computer screen, with the letter changing every half a second. The child might be instructed to "respond to the letter X, but only if it was preceded by the letter A". Thus they have to closely monitor the task and avoid distraction. In these circumstances, ADHD children typically miss a number of targets while making a number of false positives, i.e. responding to items that are not targets. The Manly et al. (2002) study is particularly interesting, in that they presented the Test of Everyday Attention for Children (TEA-Ch). This follows on the rationale of the Test of Everyday Attention (Robertson et al., 1994) and includes a number of tests in the various domains of attentional function, i.e. stimulus selection, sustained attention, and executive control. They found in a sample of ADHD children that performance was only impaired on the sustained attention task, with intact performance on the other elements.

The explanation for these types of findings has typically been in terms of inhibition (Barkley, 1999; Bayliss & Roodenrys, 2000; Nigg, 2001; Nigg et al., 2002; Perchet, Revol, Fourneret, Mauguiere, & Garcia-Larrea, 2001). Thus, ADHD children find it hard to sustain their attention on a task over a period of time because they are unable to inhibit distraction, from whatever source it may come. Distraction can be external, e.g. noticing a movement of the examiner, or internal, i.e. thinking about some other task or wish. Thus ADHD children are prone to miss targets and, when they do attend, it is quite likely that they will respond inappropriately to non-targets, as they find it difficult to inhibit an urge to respond once it is initiated. For example, Perchet et al. (2001) suggested there was a problem with the initial anticipatory response in their evoked potential study using Posner's paradigm. The exact nature of this inhibitory deficit in ADHD remains to be precisely elucidated, but it may involve quite specific processes. For example Nigg et al. (2002) found a problem with an antisaccade task (where subjects have to move their eyes in the opposite direction to a target) but not with negative priming (where irrelevant information in a visual display has to be ignored in order to respond to a target, subsequently slowing responses on following trials to the previously ignored information). Thus inhibition processes may be very specific, perhaps (as in this case) involving inhibition of responses, as opposed to inhibition of irrelevant information.

Although there is much debate as to its true merit, there is a therapeutic response available for ADHD, which involves the prescription of stimulant-type medication, such as Ritalin. Paradoxically, ADHD children receiving such medication seem to loose the hyperactive tendency and become better able to concentrate. There are studies in the literature suggesting that the performance deficits found in ADHD are ameliorated by the medication (e.g. Kempton et al., 1999). The current view is that such medication exerts its effects by acting upon dopamine pathways, located predominantly in the frontal lobes. Further support for such a view comes from Faraone and Biederman (1998). These authors suggested a genetic link in the aetiology of ADHD, implicating genes that are involved in the dopamine systems. Given that the current medical approach seems to target the frontal lobes, and given also a genetic hypothesis centring on these regions, it is perhaps unsurprising that researchers should have looked to a frontal account of ADHD. This very much mirrors the situation with schizophrenia, as described previously. As with schizophrenia, a number of studies in the literature report attempts to find deficits on frontal lobe tasks. Some of the more recent of these will be briefly considered.

Frontal deficits in ADHD

Of the more important frontal type tasks that have been outlined already in this chapter, all of them have been found to be impaired in ADHD in at least one study. Culbertson and Zillmer (1998) observed deficits on the Tower of London task, while Gansler et al. (1998) found impairment on the Trails task (which requires set switching). Cepeda, Cepeda, and Kramer (2000) also found deficits on a set switching task. Schreiber, Javorsky, Robinson, and Stern (1999) described how ADHD children had great difficulties on the Rey–Osterrieth Complex Figure test. This abstract drawing requires considerable organization to copy and reproduce, and poor disorganized attempts have traditionally been seen as reflecting poor frontal function. Clark, Prior, and Kinsella (2000) found impairments on the Six Elements task and the Hayling Sentence Completion task. As previously noted, the Six Elements task has been put forward as the quintessential frontal lobe test, requiring planning, organization, working memory, and temporal sequencing, so it would be disappointing for the frontal/ executive deficit hypothesis of ADHD if it had not been found to be impaired. Barkley et al. (2001—also Barkley et al., 1997) found that ADHD children had difficulties with temporal discounting and reproduction, both of which would be predicted by a frontal account based on known problems experienced by head-injured patients with frontal lesions. Finally, Mahone, Koth, Cutting, Singer, and Denckla (2001) found that ADHD children had deficits with both letter and semantic fluency (e.g. generating as many words as possible that begin with the letter F in 1 minute, or generating as many animals as possible). Given the above findings it is not surprising that some authors have suggested that frontal-type tasks may be useful in the assessment of ADHD (Grodzinsky & Barkley, 1999), although some authors have found them to lack sensitivity to the condition (Perugini et al., 2000). Thus it seems that deficits on frontal-type tasks are common in ADHD, but may not always be present in every case (but see the earlier discussion in Chapter 5 about how frontal function and intelligence could be linked, thus deficits may be less apparent in high IQ ADHD children). There is further support for frontal deficits in ADHD from recent neuroimaging work (Hill et al., 2003).

An executive deficits theory of ADHD

Having observed that ADHD children have difficulty on a number of frontal-type tasks, we are now confronted with the issue that was discussed at some length earlier in the chapter: Is there some core deficit that underlies the performance on all the various tasks? Or does the widespread range of impairments reflect the gross involvement of the frontal lobes in the condition?

As was noted at the start of this chapter, inability to perform sustained attention tasks, due to problems with inhibiting distraction and inappropriate responses, has been seen as quite fundamental to the condition. It is conceivable that such a deficit could underlie performance on the other frontal tasks, all of which require concentration over time and the ability to carefully monitor and tailor one's response.

One such view has already been put forward in some depth by Russell Barkley, a worker whose name has featured prominently in this chapter. In 1997, Barkley published an extensive theoretical position on the nature of deficits in ADHD. Figure 6.1 neatly summarizes Barkley's overall position.

As can be seen from the diagram, Barkley puts inhibition at the head of his theory. As he explains, it is because of this inability that a range of other executive processes become dysfunctional. It is not in his view the case that inhibition is fundamental to these other processes. Rather, it is the case that the other processes need the space in which to operate. Without such behavioural space, created by not immediately responding to a stimulus and pausing to ponder alternative responses, the other processes do not get a chance to operate. Barkley outlines four such executive processes. These are working memory, self-regulation, use of inner speech, and reconstitution. Many of the ideas outlined under these headings would be familiar to current cognitive psychologists, although there are some novel

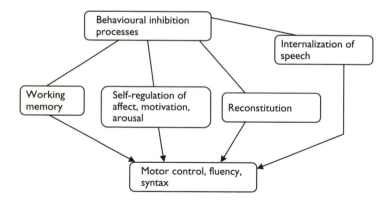

Figure 6.1 **Barkley's theory of executive deficits in attention deficit hyperactivity disorder (ADHD)**
In Barkley's model, behavioural inhibition processes underpin other executive functions, which in turn drive complex behaviours such as motor control, fluency, and syntax.

elements. For example, Barkley draws heavily on Bronowski (1977) in outlining a view of the role of inner speech in mental control and self-regulation. Cognitive psychologists have not in recent times tended to place too much emphasis on the role of inner speech in cognitive control (in the influential working memory model [Baddeley & Hitch, 1974] inner speech is simply a rehearsal medium for keeping information active). This could, however, be about to change (see Baddeley et al. [2001] for a study implicating inner speech in the control of set switching—the current author also has data suggesting inner speech is important in automating such tasks, and in other frontal tasks such as the Stroop).

In turn, in Barkley's model, these various executive functions are important in the control and mediation of motor, syntax, and fluency responses. Barkley's model also incorporates and extends Fuster's (1989) views of frontal functioning, as outlined earlier in the chapter, perhaps going further than Fuster in specifying the relationship of inhibition processes to the other executive functions.

Barkley's view of executive deficits in ADHD is refreshing in many respects. It attempts, by marshalling an impressive array of findings, to specify a range of executive processes and show how these processes interact with each other, with one aspect (inhibition) being fundamental and underpinning the other four. Deficits in these systems then lead to a range of consequences in terms of behavioural regulation. As Barkley suggests, his framework gives rise to many testable predictions and expectations. It would be interesting, for example, to follow up on the recent study of Christ, White, Brunstrom, and Abrams (2003), who reported inhibition deficits on the Stroop and reverse response tasks for children with bilateral spastic cerebral palsy. This condition leads to poor connectivity between the prefrontal cortex and other brain regions. If Barkley is correct, then the children should have other executive deficits arising from their early difficulties with inhibition. Although there are weaknesses in parts of Barkley's account (the role of inner speech is far from clear), it is apparent that other bodies of work on executive functioning could benefit from similar theoretical synthesis. Research on ADHD will no doubt play a key role in helping us to understand the complex functions of the frontal lobes.

Summary

Executive functions are thought to control and direct cognitive processing. A number of tasks are thought to tap into this aspect of our ability, in particular the Wisconsin Card Sorting task and Tower of Hanoi, along with more recent developments such as the Six Elements task. Frontal patients typically display disorganized behaviour on such tasks. They may show gross perseveration in their responses, repeating an incorrect response or sequence of responses many times. Researchers have looked for similar deficits in schizophrenia but the findings have been far from consistent, with studies arguing for and against the existence of such deficits. Part of the problem may be the lack of clarity about exactly what schizophrenia is, and whether it constitutes a single diagnostic entity. Medication is frequently a further complication in many studies. However, executive deficits have recently been described in patients with dementia, including Alzheimer's disease and especially frontotemporal dementia. In fact, the way the latter is distinguished in some classifications relies on the assessment of executive function. Such patients, and more careful study of head-injured patients with the new paradigms being developed in experimental psychology, will no doubt shed further light on this important aspect of functioning in the future. Finally, this chapter went on to outline the childhood condition of ADHD. It was suggested that there are two distinct subtypes, with the combined type showing distinctive impairments in the executive domain. The condition is thought to arise from frontal deficits, thus redemption comes from stimulant-type medication. There are deficits in performance on many frontal-type tasks and it has been suggested that impaired inhibition may be the common thread that ties together these various behavioural sequelae. This is well illustrated in Barkley's unified theory of executive deficits in ADHD. It is suggested that this model can be seen as an advance in how theories of executive function should be conceived, although it is ambitious in its reach.

At this point in time it seems premature to put forward a unified theory of executive functioning, since there is little clarity in the literature about exactly what is encompassed by this concept. Despite this, it is clear that if the area is going to progress, then some kind of model or theory is going to be needed, even if it subsequently turns out to be quite misguided. Such a model needs to move beyond the sketchy outlines that have been offered in the past, to a position where directly testable predictions can be made. It is the current author's view, therefore, that Barkley's theory of ADHD does represent progress of a sort, although cognitive purists would no doubt complain about its ambitious scale. In Chapter 8 I outline further how neural network models could help us to further progress such thinking, by showing in working simulations how interacting processes can be brought to bear on tasks to produce "executive"-type behaviour. Chapter 7, however, will deal with the remaining issue in attention, that of vigilance.

Chapter 7

Vigilance

Overview

THIS CHAPTER REVIEWS the concept of vigilance and sustained attention. A number of findings in relation to specific conditions are outlined. It is suggested that work in this area is less well developed than on other topics in attention.

Early work on vigilance

Of all the various aspects of attention that psychologists and neuroscientists have studied, vigilance has perhaps been the area least attended to. Yet this aspect of attention was probably the first to have been given serious consideration from a cognitive stance.

Early pioneering work on vigilance was carried out at the Applied Psychology Unit in Cambridge during the Second World War (Mackworth, 1950). This work is fully described in Chapter 1 and will not therefore be described again here. Suffice it to say that Mackworth found that vigilance decrements are very slow to appear, and that participants are capable of monitoring very boring and repetitive tasks for many hours before making significant lapses. Although not widely used since, Mackworth's pioneering technique is still occasionally used in research today (e.g. Giambra & Quilter, 1988, Kass, Vodanovich, Stanny, & Taylor, 2001).

The concept of vigilance and sustained attention

Mackworth's work serves as a good introduction to the concept of vigilance. "Vigilance" refers to the ability to maintain an active and alert frame of mind over extended periods of time, in the face of little external stimulation. Mackworth's early work also served to establish some basic findings, which have in practice made research on the topic difficult. Basically, people can maintain a vigil for remarkable periods of time, which makes research in the laboratory difficult. Few participants (or researchers!) are willing to spend hours in a laboratory performing routine tasks in the hope that eventually errors will appear (obviously being at war makes a big difference). Thus little concerted work has been done on the factors underlying vigilance. For example, it would be interesting to find out if there are individual differences in the extent to which people are able to stay awake. Instead, workers have tended to focus more on sustained attention. Sustained attention is the ability to maintain an efficient level of responding on a demanding task over a period of time. Typically, such tasks require frequent responses and it is possible to observe decrements in performance over a period of minutes rather than hours. Before going on to consider the evidence for deficits in sustained attention in various conditions, we will briefly review some of the suggestions being put forward regarding localization of this function.

Localization of vigilance functions

Rueckert and Grafman (1996) administered a set of three sustained attention tasks to volunteers and claimed that the right frontal lobes were implicated in the function. Similarly, Coull, Frith, Frackowiak, and Grasby (1996) identified the right frontoparietal lobes for sustained attention and the left frontoparietal lobes for maintenance of verbal material (the phonological loop aspect of the working memory model [Baddeley & Hitch, 1974]). Semba (2000) highlighted the role of the basal forebrain, while Sarter, Givens, and Bruno (2001) suggested the frontal and parietal lobes, particularly in the right hemisphere, based on a review of imaging studies. Added to numerous studies of stroke patients with sustained attention deficits following lesions to the right frontoparietal areas (see later), it seems that there is an emerging consensus that this is a crucial region for sustained attention in humans.

Conditions where sustained attention is impaired

In reviewing the range of conditions that have been documented as having sustained attention deficits, we will start with the less contentious and work our way towards the more difficult areas.

Recent reports have illustrated a clear attentional deficit in biploar disorder (Clark, Iversen, & Goodwin, 2002; Harmer, Clark, Grayson, & Goodwin, 2002). It should be noted that this is during the stages of the condition where the mood extremes have stabilized, i.e. not during extreme depression or mania. The latter study cited suggested that the deficit was fairly pure, i.e. an inability to sustain effort, rather than a deficit in working memory. There have also been suggestions of sustained attention deficits in temporal lobe epilepsy (Fleck, Shear, & Strakowski, 2001). Not unexpectedly, there are similar deficits in severe closed head injury (Loken et al., 1995) although in this case it is not clear whether this is due to localized lesions or global changes in the brain (e.g. white matter shearing). Such changes could be expected to lead to inefficient processing, i.e. a slower speed of processing and therefore more rapid fatigue (see the discussion of this in Chapter 3).

As discussed in detail in Chapter 6, children with ADHD typically show impairments in sustained attention (e.g. Barry, Klinger, Lyman, Bush, & Hawkins, 2001; Hooks, Milich, & Lorch, 1994). In this case, however, the poor performance is thought not to arise out of a genuine deficit in sustained attention but rather from a chronic inability to inhibit inappropriate responses and a failure to cope with distraction. By contrast, the inability of children who experienced prenatal exposure to cocaine to sustain attention may be a pure deficit in the ability (Bandstra, Morrow, Anthony, Accornero, & Fried, 2001).

As was mentioned in Chapter 5, there is now strong evidence to link this phenomenon with deficits in sustained attention. A number of studies have shown that rehabilitation of sustained attention can improve neglect, that this procedure produces better functional outcome, and that the right parietal lobe is implicated (Hjaltason, Tegner, Tham, & Levander, 1996; Robertson et al., 1995; Robertson et al., 1997a and b; Wilson, Manly, Coyle, & Robertson, 2000).

As has frequently been the case, the problem area for our account is schizophrenia. Given that the frontal/attention deficit account of schizophrenia has gained some currency in the last decade, it is not surprising that researchers should go looking for problems with sustained attention. A number of studies have reported the existence of such problems in patients (Cohen, Nordahl, Semple, Andreason, & Pickar, 1998; Pandurangi, Sax, Pelonero, & Goldberg, 1994; Pigache, 1999) as well as schizotypal individuals (Lenzenweger, Cornblatt, & Putnick, 1991). However, there are at least as many studies that do not find such a deficit (Cosway et al., 2002; Jones, Cardno, Sanders, Owen, & Williams, 2001; Rund, Zeiner, Sundet, Oie, & Bryhn, 1998; Schwartz, Livingston, Sautter, & Nelson, 1990). At least one study even goes completely in the opposite direction. Mar, Smith, and Sarter (1996) suggested that their patients had a problem with hyper-attention in a reward paradigm, such that they scored more hits than the controls and were more resistant to a vigilance decrement! Thus the picture in relation to schizophrenia remains far from clear. At this point in time it certainly could not be claimed that there is any consensus one way or the other for the existence of sustained attention deficits in the condition. The reasons underlying this state of affairs are probably the same as those outlined in Chapter 4. Schizophrenia is a wide-ranging condition, which may in fact be made up of a number of distinct subtypes. Furthermore, the role of medication is frequently poorly controlled. Any or all of such factors could easily account for the differences between studies.

Summary

In this chapter we have seen how the early pioneering work of Mackworth led to an early understanding of the concept of vigilance in humans but that in practical clinical situations the concept of sustained attention has proven more amenable to study. Although work on this topic is at an earlier stage than in other areas, there have been definite suggestions of conditions where this ability is affected, e.g. bipolar disorder. One of the more interesting and theoretically important observations has been the existence of sustained attention deficits in stroke patients alongside the phenomenon of unilateral left neglect. This seems to implicate the frontoparietal regions and has important implications for rehabilitation. Finally, the situation with regard to schizophrenia is far from clear, with studies both for and against the existence of such a deficit. The exact mechanisms underlying vigilance and sustained attention remain to be more fully specified and the range of conditions where this function is impaired will no doubt increase (for example, the current author is led to speculate on the possible existence of such deficits in chronic fatigue syndrome and lupus erythematosus, given his own clinical impression).

Chapter 8

Neural networks and attention

Overview

THIS CHAPTER SETS out to provide an introduction to the area of neural network models. As such, it is less ambitious than previous chapters. It would be totally beyond the scope of a single chapter to review all the attempts to model attentional phenomena that have been published in the literature. Instead, this chapter sets out to explain the basic principles, and to illustrate with one or two examples how such models have been applied within this domain. The aim of the chapter is to enable readers to grasp the fundamental principles, so that they feel confident to engage with literature in the area. Such models are likely to increase in frequency and importance in the future, and readers will therefore need to be able to read and evaluate this type of work. It is the author's view that there has been much misunderstanding of the field in recent years, in particular with many workers not understanding the exact nature of such models or what role they can play in cognitive neuropsychology. In particular, such models are frequently being presented at applied neuro-psychology conferences and there is an urgent need for this audience to become critically articulate in this area. If the reader finishes this chapter imbued with a healthy scepticism and an intention to treat such models with exactly the same degree of critical appraisal as any other theory, then this section of the book will have served its purpose.

Background

Ever since the advent of cognitive psychology in the mid-1950s, there has been a tendency to see the computer as a metaphor for the human mind. In fact, the modern desk-top computer serves as a very good metaphor. It has a "central executive" in the shape of a primary processing chip, which processes information very rapidly in a serial fashion (currently at speeds approaching several GHz). It has long-term storage device, typically in the shape of a hard drive, which currently can store many Gbytes of data. Data that will be actively used needs to be retrieved from the computer's long-term memory (hard drive) into a temporary storage area (random access memory), analogous to short-term memory. Computers that have a number of core processing chips, allowing information to be processed in parallel, are now starting to appear, which will no doubt further enhance the computer–brain metaphor.

Besides seeing the computer as a useful metaphorical device, workers have sought to harness the power of computers more directly, as a theoretical tool. Thus there have been many attempts over the years to simulate various aspects of cognition on computers. A well-known example is Marr's (1982) theory of early perceptual processing.

This area of research, where workers try to simulate cognitive processes on computers, is often referred to as artificial intelligence. Two main objectives can be distinguished within this camp. There are those who seek to enable computers to achieve complex and useful tasks, such as object recognition, and there are those who seek to explore models as a way of helping us to understand human cognition. It is the latter with which we are interested here.

Within artificial intelligence (AI), much early work focused on the use of specially developed computer languages, e.g. Prolog. Such languages had been developed with features useful to AI programmers. Thus the encoding of knowledge structures is typically advanced, allowing researchers to explore the ways in which knowledge is stored and retrieved. However, such an approach required the researcher to be very specific about how a model should work, so that the code could be generated to reflect the theory. There were many who found such models to be quite unsatisfactory, often citing lack of biological plausibility.

In the 1980s a new approach to computer modelling began to appear in psychology, with the rise of connectionism, or neural networks. The approach was given a boost with the appearance of two companion volumes by Rumelhart, McClelland, and the PDP Group (1986). In this technique, models are built up of simple neuron-like units. This gives them an immediate appearance of biological plausibility (although anyone acquainted with the full biological complexities of even a simple real neuron will quickly realize that these simulated neurons are vastly inferior!). Neural network models have many advantages over the traditional, language-based, AI approach. There is no need for specific programming. Instead, an architecture of simple neuron units is specified, and then trained. Using the technique of back propagation, in which a network is exposed to a pattern and then gradually adjusted until the required output is achieved, networks appear to learn. From exposure to a number of patterns, they gradually learn a set of required outputs, which are linked to a paired set of inputs. Again, this property is appealing to psychologists because the brain is thought to sensitize itself to the environment in a similar way during development (although the number of steps required to train a neural network reduces the biological plausibility because we can't be sure how many steps the brain takes in its early sensitization).

In recent years, neural network models have been put forward representing cognitive theories in a variety of domains. For example, Plaut and Shallice (1993) put forward a model of reading, which they claimed could provide insight into the condition of dyslexia when lesioned. This has been a common methodological tactic in this field, the development of a model of normal functioning, which when damaged in particular ways reproduces the behaviour of patients.

In this chapter we are going to consider the basics of simple feed-forward neural networks, trained with back propagation techniques. There are other types of network but this is the main type used in many simulation studies. We are then going to look briefly at how such networks might be used to simulate behaviour within the attentional domain, taking models of frontal-type tasks as an example (modelling executive function may not seem the easiest place to start but in fact the models to date have been relatively straightforward since such tasks can be easily specified in terms of expected outcomes and required responses). Our purpose here is not to achieve a full knowledge of all neural network research in this area but to enable readers to gain some insight into the method. In particular, it is hoped to demonstrate the problems, pitfalls and limitations of the approach, so that readers will be able to access work in this field with a critical eye.

Basic principles of neural networks

In the early years of neural network research, workers experimented with simple models of connected neuron-like units, connected together in layers, which might be trained to recognize an input pattern and give a particular response. Initially, such models consisted of two layers, and these early models met with some success (Minsky & Papert, 1988). However, there were problems with these early models, in that there were certain patterns that they simply could not be trained to recognize. This stalled development for a while, until it was realized that the addition of a third "hidden" layer, in between the main input and output layers would solve the problem (see Figure 1.11). This simple addition seemed to open up the prospect that such models could now be trained to recognize all kinds of complex patterns and relationships in data, and transform the data to give all kinds of responses. Thus researchers realized that the models could be turned to all kinds of problems, and the connectionist revolution had commenced.

The units these models are made up of are said to be "neuron"-like in a very general sense. As information flows through a network, the units receive inputs from neurons in previous layers. Each unit sums the activation arriving from the previous layer, and itself becomes activated in proportion to the amount of incoming "excitation". The unit then itself passes on this level of activation to all units in the following layer, which again is summed by the following set of units leading to their activation. As with real neurons, input units are activated in an all-or-none fashion and the eventual output pattern is also coded in terms of all-or-none activation. (However hidden units do not necessarily activate in an all-or-none fashion, leading to a breakdown in the analogy—it might be better simply to see the hidden layer as a way of computationally implementing neuronal summation.)

These simple neural network models are capable of solving all kinds of problems. A very simple example is the XOR network (Figure 8.1). This simple network consists of two input units and one output unit, with a hidden layer of two units. The network can be successfully trained to discriminate patterns of input where all input units are either active or inactive (i.e. 1,1 or 0,0) from patterns where

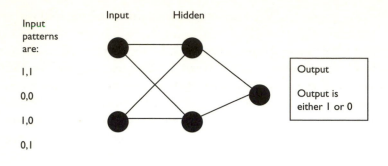

Figure 8.1 **The simple XOR network**
The model is trained to distinguish between patterns where the inputs are
the same (i.e. 1,1 or 0,0) and patterns where they are different (1,0 or 0,1).

one unit is active and the other not (1,0, or 0,1). While it seems a very
simple problem, and the network can easily achieve this, this is in
fact an example of a problem that requires a hidden layer. The early,
two-layer models could not achieve this simple discrimination; a
hidden layer is required to make the transformation. After training,
the various connections between the units have particular values, such
that the inputs to the model, multiplied by the connection weights and
fed through the network, will produce activation in the subsequent
layers and eventually result in the required output. Thus, when the
XOR network is input 1,1 or 0,0, the output node activates to 1,
whereas when 1,0 or 0,1 are input the final output node activates to 0.

How do we actually arrive at the situation where we have a fully
trained model, with the connecting weights between units set at values,
which will result in the required output? In some instances it is possible
to work them out by hand but in any large model this would be
impossible. (Incidentally, there is no good rule to determine for any
particular model how big the hidden layer should be—if the model
works then it is big enough, but it should not be too big, as this would
lead to redundancy and inefficiency.) Fortunately, a technique has
been devised to allow the models to set themselves up using a trial and
error process. The patterns the network is required to recognize are
presented to the network, and the information allowed to feed
forward, initially using random weights for the connections. This will

lead to a random degree of activation at the output units. The degree of error at each output unit is then calculated and this error is then fed backwards through the network, adjusting each connection by a small amount in proportion to the amount of error which that connection was associated with. This is done successively for all the patterns the network needs to learn and, little by little, the output for each pattern moves in the required direction until eventually all the input patterns are producing the required outputs. At that point the network is said to be trained, and the connection weights are saved for future reference.

Hopefully, by this point you are starting to get a feel for what these neural network models involve. Having illustrated a simple case, through the XOR example, we can make a few general points that will apply to more complex models as well. First of all, notice that whatever inputs are given to these models, it has to be encoded in simple 0,1 binary patterns (it is possible actually to use models with variable inputs between 0 and 1 but this detracts from the biological plausibility we are trying to achieve). So whatever the input is, it needs to be put into 0,1 codes. In many models, this is achieved in highly implausible ways, for the sake of quickly getting the model up and running. For example, if we want to model human reading, we would need to somehow code for letters in particular positions. Let's say we want our model to read simple three-letter words such as "cat". The model needs to be able to input letters in three positions. There are 26 letters in the alphabet, so a simple way to code each letter would be to use a number from 1 to 26, and our model needs this in binary, so five neurons will be needed to represent the number in binary (e.g. "a" is 00001, and "z" is 11010). We thus have the model illustrated in Figure 8.2, which we can present with any three-letter word. Let's imagine that the model is activating semantic features, so the word cat activates "has fur", "meows", and "has four legs". The other features illustrated relate to the word "hat".

From the above discussion and illustration, it can be seen that inputs can easily be encoded into the required binary format, although this seems highly implausible. The answer to this criticism (i.e. lack of plausibility) is that we are trying to see how concepts can be represented in a network, and not to reproduce in an accurate sense the human visual system. If we were trying to achieve a more plausible

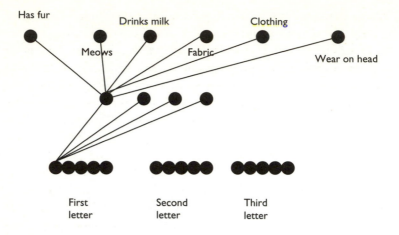

Figure 8.2 **A simple model of reading**
In this simple model of semantic activation from words, the first three output-layer concepts relate to "cat", while the last three relate to "hat". Only connections from the first neuron in each layer are shown, which is a common convention.

input then we could simply expand the input layer, perhaps using grids to code letters, in a system reminiscent of the human retina. Perhaps, however, this simply complicates the model unnecessarily, and the shorthand representation given previously could suffice.

At the same time, the outputs used in typical models are also highly suspect. For example, in the simple reading model given here, output concepts are represented by a single unit. It is highly unlikely that semantic concepts in the brain depend on a single neuron! Yet many models are not much more elaborate than this (even if we expand on this several hundred-fold, using big clusters of units in the output layer, we are still unlikely to be approaching the biological reality of a brain made up of billions of neurons [each with thousands of connections of many different types]).

In our simple reading model, then, concepts are activated in response to a word input. Of course, in real life we need to get some sort of response from our participants, e.g. by them actually reading out loud the word. We can achieve this by simply adding on top a second neural network, which surveys the feature concepts activated and identifies the word to be output (Figure 8.3). We can imagine that the output units now represent the phonological pattern to be produced. (We will not complicate matters for the time being by considering the different routes to reading, e.g. grapheme to phoneme conversion, suffice it to say that our model is simply of the semantic reading route, thought to operate in some circumstances, e.g. in deep dyslexia).

Imagine that we train our model to recognize a small number of words, e.g. "cat", "dog", "bat", "hat", "mat", and "tap". Three of these words will be quite distinctive, having semantic properties shared by few other words e.g. "controls water" in the case of tap. On the other hand, cat and dog will share many properties in common, e.g. "has four legs". Thus if our model is damaged in some way, we might predict that those words sharing a number of semantic properties will be more likely to be confused. Thus we might predict

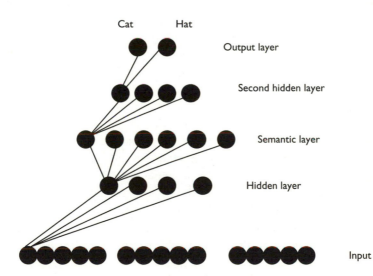

Figure 8.3 **A more complex model of reading**
In this modular network, the first network activates stored features and the second network then identifies the semantic concept, which can then be used to produce a response. Such a model might account for the man-made living distinction observed on object naming tasks in some patients, since living things will be less distinctive and share more features.

that a damaged model will have more trouble with the living things than with the man-made objects. We would be predicting that deep dyslexic patients might make the same kinds of errors in reading that many anomic patients make when trying to name pictures. This would further support the view that the man-made/living distinction arose out of properties of the semantic system as opposed to the visual properties of the objects themselves.

A number of points can be made from the extension of our example above. First of all, an important part of any particular model is the set of patterns used to train it and the type of outputs specified. An often overlooked feature of such models is that the order in which patterns are presented during training can actually make a difference to the way the model becomes organized. A further point is that the way that such models are analysed following damage is quite arbitrary. If we damage a model such as that in our more complex reading example, the likelihood is that the damage will cause units in the output layer to become less clear in terms of activation. We then have to assume that this clouding of the pattern will be dealt with by the system somehow, leading to changes in behaviour such as a slowing in reaction time (in fact it is a very simple matter to devise a decision-making network that can be added on to the output layer, such that unclear patterns are resolved towards the closest match). If the damage is extensive then the model may make the wrong decision, in effect saying the wrong word, which in this case would be a semantic error. Getting networks to behave in this manner typically requires extensive damage! In the author's experience, a simple network such as this may require at least 40% of the connections to be disrupted before it makes significant errors of this type.

Some final points to note before we move on to discuss networks in relation to attention. First, as mentioned above, neural networks are remarkably robust. They require considerable amounts of damage before they start to go substantially wrong. Second, they have remarkable powers of generalization, i.e. given a comprehensive set of data they are capable of giving sensible responses to inputs they have never encountered before. This property is now being widely exploited, e.g. in the financial sector. If you can find a way of adequately encoding the behaviour of the stock market over the last 20 years, there is a fair chance that your network will be able to make reasonable predictions about which shares are likely to rise and fall tomorrow.

On a theoretical note, it is worth bearing in mind that for any particular problem there are likely to be a number of different neural network architectures that could encode that problem (not to mention any number of different types of neural network). Any number of input and output units could be used, depending on how one chooses to represent the data, and the size of the hidden layer is fairly arbitrary. It is becoming increasingly common for network models to be built in a modular fashion, although one could decide to run several types of input through the same hidden layer. For example, in our model of reading, if we wanted to add-in the effects of context this could be done in several ways, and we could choose whether this additional variable will influence the initial input network, the output network, or both. When we lesion a model, this can be done in many different ways by removing connections or units in this or that layer. Different lesion sites may well lead to what looks like the same network behaviour. The point of all this is that designing a particular network in a particular way, showing that it can then simulate a behaviour, and furthermore that damage leads to impaired performance reminiscent of patients, by itself actually proves very little. There has been a tendency in the past for newcomers to the field to believe that a successful neural network model, in and of itself, could offer powerful support for a particular theoretical view of how the brain might operate. In fact it does no such thing. Any number of different models, lesioned in countless different ways, could produce exactly the same or very similar patterns of performance. At the most, all that neural network models probably really show is that it is possible to devise a neural network in that way that appears to simulate that particular behaviour. Full stop. Given this, how then should we evaluate neural networks? The important point is that neural networks, as they currently exist, are nothing more than a theoretical device. In the same way that cognitive psychologists use box and arrow diagrams to explain their theories, neural networks are simply another way of expressing a theory. As such, they should be evaluated in the same way as any other theory. In what ways do they advance our understanding? Do they explain all the available data? Do they generate new predictions? If they add very little to our

ATTENTION

understanding on top of what can be gained from the simpler diagrammatic explanations, then all the effort has probably not been worthwhile. Despite these reservations, it is the current author's view that neural networks can help us to advance our thinking considerably. For one thing they require us to think much more clearly and precisely about what is happening than traditional theories have encouraged us to do. No neural network theory of working memory, for example, can leave a whole space, loosely labelled as "the central executive", unfilled. Also, because they require a much finer level of detail and specification in our theorizing they are likely to generate predictions that would otherwise not have been made. They also make us think much more closely about how systems develop, and how particular training regimes might lead to particular consequences. Bearing all this in mind, we will now move on to consider a few applications within the domain of attention.

Modelling control processes

Frontal-type tasks are generally well specified with clear responses required, and thus it is perhaps not too surprising that several early attempts to develop neural network models in the attention arena have chosen this aspect of behaviour. So, for example, Dehaene and Changeux (1991) presented a neural network model of Wisconsin card sorting behaviour. This is a fairly straightforward model, similar to one devised by the current author as an example for teaching neural network principles, Ward (1997a). I will refer here to my own version, as it will allow greater detail of exposition (Figure 8.4) (for an explanation of the principles underlying the Wisconsin card sorting task, see Chapter 7).

The model illustrated takes advantage of a recent trend within neural network modelling, the use of feedback (Bechtel, 1993). Thus the output from the model is fed back and entered into the input on successive stages of processing, the assumption being that each time the model tries to sort a card correctly, it will cycle through the network again. Thus the model has a memory (which is probably akin to working memory since it is maintained by cycling through

NEURAL NETWORKS AND ATTENTION

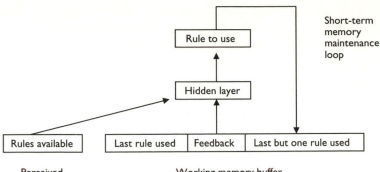

***Figure 8.4* A model of Wisconsin card sorting behaviour**
This neural network can perform the Wisconsin Card Sorting task. Individual neurons are not shown and connections between layers are represented by a single arrow. As can be seen, the model has a working memory buffer and makes use of a feedback loop.

processing stages, whereas long-term memory could be assumed to be represented in the connection weights between units). The input to the model is the characteristics of the current card to be sorted, i.e. the shape, colour, and number it represents. The output is the rule to be used for sorting this card. The feedback loop maintains information about the last rule used, and whether it was correct or incorrect. The model is trained by presenting it with all the stimulus cards and telling it what response it should make if the last rule used was correct or incorrect. For the model to work perfectly, it needs to maintain in its feedback loop, the outcome of the last two attempts at sorting. Thus if it used number the time before last and it was incorrect, and it used shape last time and it was incorrect, then this time it should use colour, the only remaining valid rule. If the model retains only the last move, then it is possible for it to get into a perseverative cycle, alternating constantly between each of two rules, e.g. responding colour, shape, colour, shape, instead of switching to number. This in fact is reminiscent of what many normal control subjects do, suggesting that this behaviour in some participants could be due to a failure to maintain more than just the last move in working memory. If the feedback loop is removed or damaged, then the model behaves exactly as a frontal lobe patient does, making continuous perservative responses.

This model seems somewhat unsatisfactory in many ways. It does not seem to capture what we tend to think of as "executive functioning". Human subjects, when they come to do the Wisconsin Card Sorting task, are briefly told the instructions and then they get on with it, usually in a very creditable fashion, whereas our model has had to be laboriously taught, through a very long training cycle, exactly what it should do on any particular occasion. Also, we tend to think of executive processes as being very general, able to be brought to bear on a variety of tasks, whereas this model only deals with the Wisconsin Card Sorting task. Also, the model seems rather descriptive, it fails to really address crucial issues, such as how does the short-term memory component really work? Is it based on a copy of the previous response stored in a buffer, or on activation of the existing concept in long-term memory? Why do patients fail to address the working memory buffer? How exactly does the system fail? Clearly there is much left to be answered, but at least the model gets us thinking about a range of issues we might not otherwise have addressed.

To deal with some of these dissatisfactions with the above model, the current author devised a much more sophisticated attempt (Ward, 1997a). This also makes use of feedback and also the growing trend towards modularity in such models (Bechtel, 1993; McCloskey, 1991). Unlike the previous model, this version had to be general purpose, i.e. would use the same framework to illustrate behaviour on a variety of "frontal" tasks. The tasks chosen were the Stroop (Perret, 1974), the Tower of Hanoi (Shallice, 1988), and again the Wisconsin Card Sorting task (Flashman, et al., 1991). Also, the model had to make use of the generalization property of neural networks to solve the tasks, i.e. the network was to be trained in general principles but not specifics. Thus, in relation to the Wisconsin Card Sorting task, the network was trained to recognize the input cards. It was also trained to sort the cards according to the possible rules. It was further trained to try a different rule if it was told that a rule was incorrect. It was not, however, trained exhaustively on every possible Wisconsin stimulus card. Similarly, the network was trained so that it could perceive (i.e. receive input and activate semantic concepts around) the problem space of the Tower of Hanoi. Thus it knew about discs, disc size, and pegs. It was trained to activate certain principles in response to verbal instructions, e.g. "move the discs from left to right", "don't repeat a move just made", and "move the biggest disc possible". For the Stroop task, words elicited both the word and colour concept, with the model implicitly being biased towards the reading response. To overcome this required activation of an "inhibition" process, such that the colour was output in preference to the word.

Thus, looking at the model (Figure 8.5) it can be seen that there are in effect four separate neural networks working together to achieve the various tasks. To begin with, one network is responsible for encoding the current problem space, causing an internal representation of the problem domain to be activated, e.g. which discs are currently on which pegs in the Tower of Hanoi. A second network, presumably activated on the basis of instructions given verbally, activates certain concepts that can be used to constrain processing, e.g. use feedback, move discs to the right, sort cards according to a rule. A third network conveys the results of the previous round of processing, in a working memory loop, causing an internal representation of the last responses and feedback to be maintained in the internal representations (and presumably maintaining problem set as well). Finally, a response network takes all the internal activations and generates a response. Prior to this, however, there is an internal iterative process (the model gets the chance to go "hmmmm. . ."). This was included primarily to facilitate performance on the Tower of Hanoi task, where several candidate moves need to be evaluated against each other, in the light of task constraints.

It was found that the general purpose framework was indeed able to accomplish the goals set, i.e. to produce valid responses on the three tasks. It should be noted that the network was trained only in the three domains in terms of general principles, i.e. it was not coached on each and every response. Thus on the Tower of Hanoi, having learned the two principles "move the largest disc possible as far to the right as possible" and "don't immediately undo a move just made", the model solved the three-disc problem in nine moves (like a human novice it fails to look several moves ahead and thus is slightly inefficient— looking ahead would require the model to cycle through the response

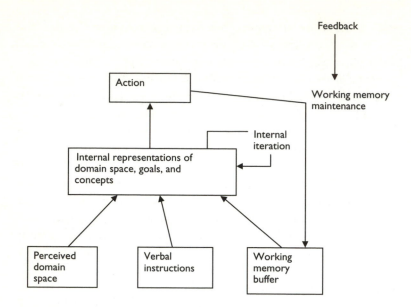

Figure 8.5 **A general neural network model of complex executive function**
Various types of input converge on an internal representation, and an iterative process is then used to produce candidate responses (such an iterative
process is particularly necessary for tasks such as the Tower of Hanoi, where
several possible moves have to be considered). The suggested action is then
remembered in working memory via a feedback loop. Note that although
this diagram looks like a traditional cognitive theory, it was actually imple-
mented in a computerized neural network. A further interesting point about
the network is that no single process can be labelled a central executive.
Rather, it is the application of a given set of rules to a particular domain
space, plus the making use of memory for past moves and feedback, which
results in executive behaviour.

network several times, holding potential responses in the short-
term memory buffer for consideration). It could be said that, like the
previous model, this one also required extensive training on the
tasks to be able to input the problem domains and operate the general
principles, whereas a human subject gets down to the task after one
hearing of the instructions. In fact this latter view is not correct.
Although "executive" tasks are often said to be novel, in reality what is
novel is simply the way in which various concepts have to be brought to

bear on the problem domain. There is no such thing as a totally novel task, because if it was genuinely 100% novel you would not be able to do it. If I ask you how many hurglies can you fit inside a dolery, you are at a loss as to how to even start (the answer, by the way, is three). When it comes to the Tower of Hanoi, you come to the task armed with a knowledge of what a disc is, how one object can be bigger than another, what "move a disc" means, and so on. All of this knowledge was acquired laboriously during development. In a sense, then, all we are doing in the general training of the current network is allowing it to catch up on all that development. Having done that it can then apply the general principles it has learned to the various tasks.

When lesioned, the network behaves in ways reminiscent of frontal patients on each of the three tasks. The exact errors produced depend on which of the four networks has been lesioned. For example, damaging the working memory loop leads to perseveration, damaging the verbal activation of general principles leads to a failure to carry out the instructions correctly (e.g. reading errors on the Stroop), and damaging the response mechanism leads to various idiosyncratic errors, especially on the Wisconsin Card Sorting task. The model leads us to consider some novel ideas within executive functioning, for example the exact role of language in control (as put forward by Vygotsky and recently revived by Baddeley et al., 2001). It also might lead to greater consideration of the role of individual developmental histories and the extent to which this leads general control principles being available to individuals to different extents.

Clearly this model has similarities to Baddeley's theory of working memory (Baddeley & Hitch, 1974) in that there is an important role for some sort of working memory buffer that retains information about previous responses and feedback. However, unlike Baddeley's working memory model, there is no "central executive". Instead, the functions ascribed to the central executive are carried out by a range of separate processes working together. Verbal instructions activate control codes, which together with information retained in the working memory buffer, act to constrain further stages of processing. The model therefore is much closer to Shallice's (1988) notion of a supervisory attentional system. According to this view, the cognitive processing system is predisposed to respond to stimuli in certain ways, according to habit and experience. To deviate from these habitual ways of responding to the world requires activation of alternative control mechanisms to constrain processing. In fact, the model outlined here is very similar to the recent one proposed by Gilbert and Shallice (2002), which also uses feedback, and "response context", i.e. a representation of the current task goal. There are clearly emerging trends within the connectionist paradigm.

Thus, we have seen how, using the principles of modularity and feedback, it is possible to build a general purpose neural network that can generalize from training based on general principles to solve frontal-type tasks. It remains to be seen whether additional tasks can be accommodated within this framework but there is no reason to see why not. For example, task switching could easily be added by adding in a "switching" concept, which would utilize the short-term memory buffer to alternate between two separate rules. Switching costs could thus arise from a variety of sources, including the extra processing required from the additional step in consulting working memory stores, through to the ambiguity imposed upon the response selection mechanism by having two rules activated simultaneously. As was indicated earlier, any neural network model should be evaluated based on the extent to which it accounts for the data, but more importantly the extent to which it encourages us to think about issues we might not otherwise have touched upon. Given the range of suggestions outlined above, this model seems to admirably serve this purpose.

To conclude, in this chapter we have covered the basic principles of neural network models and reviewed some specific examples of how they have been applied in trying to help us to understand behaviour on frontal tasks. General principles have been outlined against which such models can be evaluated. It is suggested that in future such models are likely to be modular and utilize feedback to capture important aspects of human cognition. As such, they will closely resemble the traditional box and arrow theories but will encourage us to think much more precisely about what goes on inside the boxes and how exactly the arrows are enabled to move.

Summary

In the last two decades a new style of simulation technique has arisen from within AI research, based on building models from simple, neuron-like units. Such models have come to be widely used within the discipline of psychology and are being increasingly applied to the phenomenon of attention. Early attempts at such models included the simulation of frontal-type tasks. In the future, such models may be increasingly modular, recognizing the specialization that takes place in different brain regions. They will also use feedback to capture the dynamism of the human cognitive system. While such theories often appear complex, and can be intuitively appealing and theoretically seductive, such models should be evaluated in the same terms as any other theory. They should adequately and parsimoniously explain the available data, highlight issues which require further clarification, and generate testable predictions.

Chapter 9

Future directions

ATTENTION

Overview

THIS CHAPTER BRIEFLY attempts to look forward and speculate where future research is likely to lead in further attempting to
elucidate the neuropsychology of attention.

Looking forward

Trying to predict the future is a dangerous occupation but it seems
appropriate at the end of a book like this to look forward and envisage
where research is likely to lead us. We are, of course, on fairly solid
ground if we base our speculation on those issues where further
research is apparently warranted.

   We started out our exploration of attention with the general
issue of speed of processing. As was suggested in Chapter 4, although
this is a widely used concept, little thought to date has gone into
precisely specifying exactly what the term means. For example, the
Paced Auditory Serial Addition task (PASAT) is being widely adopted
as a key outcome measure in multiple sclerosis. Leaving aside the
various questions over the validity of this test, it is clearly a complex
task. Patients have to keep in mind several numbers, add them, shout
out the sum, listen out for next number, etc. It is what might be termed
a "working memory" task, involving several subsystems of the working memory model (if not all of them!). So what exactly do we mean
to say when we claim this is a good test of speed of processing? Is
speed of processing a general system property of the brain, such that
all processes are affected to an equal degree? Or are some processes
more affected than others? And are the vulnerable processes those
that we might call "control" as opposed to "automatic". The future
will no doubt see further clarification of this issue, and perhaps some
resolution of the question as to how much deficits in other apparent
functional domains are in fact simply due to impaired speed of
processing.

   In terms of the different aspects of attention, there is a definite
trend towards the increasing use of scanning methodologies. We can
therefore look forward to increasingly precise specification of the

localization of particular functions. As scanning techniques become more refined, and are coupled with the latest techniques from experimental cognitive psychology, we can also expect processes to be fractionated to an ever finer degree, and their components localized. Thus we may in future be able to specify exactly where in the brain selective attention takes place, but also precisely which part is responsible for attending to verbal stimuli, and which part to visual. Within these we may be able to further specify exactly where different types of stimuli are processed, e.g. voices versus sounds versus tones. At these microlevels of specification we might come upon surprising levels of individual differences (indeed, such individual differences in brain localization may one day impose a limit on the ability to localize ever finer degrees of functioning).

The new scanning methodologies may also help us to shed new light upon the various conditions around which there is uncertainty. Schizophrenia in particular remains unclear in terms of the exact nature of any attentional disturbance. Using the latest paradigms developed in attention research, with schizophrenic patients undergoing scanning, could be very revealing. Comparison with controls should give a more precise idea of which areas are over- or underactive, and how medication affects this. The latest atypical antipsychotic medications are known to have a significant cognitive enhancement potential, and future research may reveal to what extent this is an important facet of such medication. If the medication appears to improve certain aspects of cognition, and if these improvements in cognition correlate with therapeutic benefits, then this might constitute some evidence that the cognitive processes were intrinsically involved in the aetiology of the condition. As things stand right now, there are many suggestions in the literature that patients with schizophrenia have deficits in various aspects of attention, including selection, executive functioning, and vigilance. What remains very unclear, despite many years of research effort, is how closely these deficits are bound up with the psychotic features of the disease. Researchers in search of the cognitive holy grail may do well to consider more closely how psychotic features such as paranoia are likely to be linked to basic cognitive processes. Furthermore, what is required to answer these questions convincingly are good longitudinal studies, starting when participants are presymptomatic. This could probably only be done as part of either a large community cohort study, or on the basis of genetic markers being used to target susceptible individuals at an early age. Given all the difficulties, my prediction would be that none of this is going to happen in the near future.

One topic in attention that we seem to be very early in the course of exploring is executive functioning (although related work has been going on under other headings, such as problem solving). Current theories of executive function will no doubt be fleshed out in the future as we explore the exact nature and relationships between different tasks thought to tap this aspect. It should become clearer whether executive function involves a core skill or is in fact made up of several independent abilities. Whether inhibition plays a crucial underpinning role and whether attention deficit hyperactivity disorder should be considered a "dysexecutive" condition will become clearer. The exact role of language in executive control may also come in for more attention. Clearly, language is very important in control functions, since everyday participants in our psychology laboratories listen to complex task instructions and then proceed to carry them out with little difficulty after only one hearing. Somehow, sophisticated control codes can be harnessed through the simple expedient of verbal instruction. Whether verbal control codes are important for ongoing task execution remains to be seen, but there is already evidence of such a role in switching at least. Closer examination of aphasic patients and patients with dementia could be informative.

On a theoretical level, it seems unlikely that the unitary notion of a central executive is likely to stand the test of time. The notion of a central executive has been one of the most unsatisfactory features of the working memory model (Baddeley & Hitch, 1974) and most researchers have realized that this label is simply being applied to a whole set of issues that are desperately in need of greater elucidation. Shallice's (1988) notion of the supervisory attentional system has had more to commend it in that at least it begins to address the issue of how attention is directed on a moment-by-moment basis. The key issue, though, of how these automated processes are interrupted according to novel and demanding task features, remains unresolved. Future research will lead to a more complex view in which a number of executive processes are put forward, served by different regions of the frontal lobes and interacting in ways as yet to be specified. At this point in time it seems that inhibition is a strong candidate for being one of the more fundamental of these.

The exact role of attention in dementia will be further explored, with executive functions receiving much closer scrutiny than they have in the past. It seems quite likely that various attentional tasks may come to be seen as important diagnostic indicators for differentiating between dementias with different aetiologies. Lewy body dementia in particular seems to involve a rapid fluctuation in attention, and tests that can reliably tap this feature may help to distinguish it from Alzheimer's disease. At the moment, such differentiation relies on the judgement of the clinician, with the suspicion that only specialist centres that routinely make the diagnosis are confident in the distinction.

Finally, as vigilance comes to be more routinely assessed by clinicians the role of this important function in various conditions will come to be more fully appreciated. Localization to the parietal lobes and relationship to unilateral neglect will come to be more fully described. The nature of unilateral neglect itself will come to be more fully appreciated, with some clarification and unification among the various competing theories.

Neural network theories will be further developed, which will advance understanding and cause researchers to focus more clearly on issues that had previously been neglected. Such developments in the general areas of attention such as selection are likely to take place within the context of more general network theories, designed to tackle more general tasks. For example, an object recognition programme could be coupled with an attentional system so that it can prioritize what it attends to. (It is easy to see the practical applications of such systems—imagine, for example, surveillance cameras that can scan a busy market place and home-in on suspicious activities!)

Finally, with the increasing numbers of clinical psychologists choosing to specialize in the exciting and important area of neuropsychology, our increased understanding of attention will lead to a variety of effective strategies for the rehabilitation of attention deficits in all kinds of disorders. Such work may come to be coupled with important advances in neuroscience, such as the implantation of neuronal material or the use of nerve growth factors that may be able to stimulate the growth of new nerves. In the decades ahead, psychologists will continue to play a key role in helping patients to maximize their degree of functioning during rehabilitation, which, coupled with emerging technologies, may allow people with even quite severe pathologies by today's standards to return to near premorbid levels of functioning.

Summary

This brief chapter looks to the future and sees progress likely to come on a number of fronts. Hazy concepts such as speed of processing will be refined, and areas that are at an early stage of development, such as executive functioning, more fully fleshed out. Scanning will lead to increasing knowledge of localization of function and greater understanding of previously problematic conditions such as schizophrenia. Finally, efforts at rehabilitation will lead to an increasing array of strategies that can be used with patients suffering from all types of attentional impairment.

Glossary

Alzheimer's disease is the most common type of senile dementia, associated with a distinctive pathology of senile plaques and neurofibrillary tangles in the brain.

Anomic is the inability to name pictures. A condition that arises from certain types of brain damage, particularly when the left hemisphere is affected.

Attention deficit hyperactivity disorder (ADHD) is a common problem in childhood where children have difficulty concentrating and staying still. May persist into adolescence and adulthood in some cases.

Automatic processing relates to processes involved in carrying out well learned, fluent tasks. Requires little overt attention, e.g. reading in skilled adult readers, driving in experienced drivers (see also controlled processing).

Central executive is a theoretical construct used in cognitive psychology to represent control processes. Deficits are sometimes referred to as "dysexecutive".

Choice reaction time is the time it takes a participant to respond to a stimulus when there are several possible stimuli that might be presented and a discrimination response is required. Thought to reflect processes involved in target detection and identification (see also simple reaction time).

Control is a comparison group used in scientific studies. Thus, if we wish to look at the effects of brain damage on task performance, we would compare patients with a group of non-brain-damaged controls (often medical patients, to allow for aspects of medicalization such as anxiety).

Controlled processing relates to processes involved in carrying out difficult, novel, and attention-demanding tasks. It is considered synonymous with consciousness by some theorists (see also automatic processing).

Covert attention is the ability to move attention around the visual field, without moving the eyes. In lay terms the ability to "look out of the corner of one's eye".

Deep dyslexia see dyslexia.

Dementia is a global intellectual decline, often as a result of neuro-degenerative disorders in old age, such as Alzheimer's disease. Thought to affect about 5% of those aged 65 and over and 20% of those aged over 85.

Dissociation is the situation where a patient can do task A but not task B (see also double dissociation).

Double dissociation is the situation where one patient can do task A but not B, and a second patient can't do A but can do B. Suggests that tasks A and B are independent processes, and the dissociation is not simply due to task difficulty or complexity.

Dual task relates to having to perform two concurrent tasks. Usually results in a decrement in performance.

Dysexecutive see central executive.

Dyslexia difficulty reading. Deep dyslexia is a term applied to some patients who make particular, semantic errors, e.g. reading cat for dog.

Evoked response potentials (ERPS) are the change in voltage across the surface of the scalp resulting from the presentation of a stimulus.

Executive see central executive.

Factor analysis is a complex statistical technique that seeks to identify similarities between sets of variables, which are then used to describe factors. Frequently used in test development, to inform and validate views on what the tests measure.

Functional nuclear magnetic resonance imaging (fMRI) is a sophisticated brain-scanning technique based on radio frequency techniques. It yields high-resolution images of internal organs.

Frontal lobes comprise the frontal one-third of the brain, immediately above the occipital cavities.

Lesion is the site of brain damage. The term can also be used to refer to the process of removing connections or units in a connectionist neural network.

Lewy body dementia is a type of senile dementia in which the prominent brain pathology consists of Lewy bodies. Currently thought to represent bout 20% of cases of senile dementia (see also Alzheimer's disease and dementia).

Lupus erythematosus is an autoimmune disease that affects the circulatory system and has neurological implications.

Modularity is the view that there are separate and discrete cognitive processes.

Neglect is the clinical condition experienced by many stroke patients whereby the side of the visual field opposite to the lesion site is "neglected", i.e. ignored. Usually only one side is affected, leading to the term "unilateral" neglect. Left neglect, caused by right lesions, can be prolonged in duration, whereas right neglect frequently resolves.

Saccade is an eye movement, from one point to the next. Our eyes are constantly moving as we change the focus of our attention in the visual field, with each movement being one saccade.

Schizophrenia is a major mental disorder in which patients experience auditory hallucinations, delusions, and paranoia. It is thought to involve the dopamine systems in frontal brain areas. The aetiology has frequently been controversial and remains unclear.

Selective attention is the ability to focus on a particular stimulus, and not be distracted by other stimuli.

Sensitivity is the ability of a test to discriminate patients from controls. Usually measured in terms of both false positives (controls who are misclassified as patients) and false negatives (patients who are looked over).

Simple reaction time is the speed with which a participant can respond to a single stimulus, without having to make any stimulus discrimination. It is also thought to reflect arousal processes (see also choice reaction time).

Speed of processing is the notion that brain processing takes place at a particular speed and that this can be indexed by performance on certain kinds of task requiring manipulation of information.

Theory of mind is the belief that other humans have a mind similar to one's own, with their own set of beliefs and views. It implies that other people's view of the world and its current status may differ to one's own. Thought to be impaired in conditions such as autism.

Transparency is the notion that behaviour reflects the workings of an underlying cognitive system.

Unilateral neglect see neglect.

Vigilance is the ability to pay attention over long periods of time in the presence of low levels of stimulation, e.g. in long-distance lorry drivers working overnight.

References

Alderman, N. (1996). Central executive deficit and response to operant conditioning methods. *Neuropsychological Rehabilitation*, 6, 161–186.

Alderman, N., Burgess, P.W., Knight, C., & Henman, C. (2003). Ecological validity of a simplified version of the multiple errands shopping test. *Journal of the International Neuropsychological Society*, 9, 31–44.

Alderman, N., & Ward, A. (1991). Behavioural treatment of the dysexecutive syndrome: Reduction of repetitive speech using response cost and cognitive overlearning. *Neuropsychological Rehabilitation*, 1, 65–80.

Allain, P., Etcharry-Bouyx, F., & Le Gall, D. (2001). A case study of selective impairment of the central executive component of working memory after a focal frontal lobe damage. *Brain and Cognition*, 45, 21–43.

Allport, D.A., Antonis, B., & Reynolds, P. (1972). On the division of attention: A disproof of the single channel hypothesis. *Quarterly Journal of Experimental Psychology, 24,* 225–235.

Allport, A., Styles, E.A., & Hsieh, S. (1994). Shifting intentional set: Exploring the dynamic control of tasks. In C. Umilta & M. Moscovitch (Eds.), *Attention and performance XV* (pp. 421–452). Cambridge, MA: MIT Press.

Amieva, H., Lafont, S., Dartigues, J.F., & Fabrigoule, C. (1999). Selective attention in Alzheimer's disease: Analysis of errors in Zazzo's Cancellation task. *Brain and Cognition, 40,* 26–29.

Amir, T., Alghara, T., Aldhari, M., Alhassani, A., Bahry, G., & Alshibani, F. (2001). Effects of caffeine on vigilance performance in introvert and extravert noncoffee drinkers. *Social Behavior and Personality, 29,* 617–624.

Archibald, C.J., & Fisk, J.D. (2000). Information processing efficiency in patients with multiple sclerosis. *Journal of Clinical and Experimental Neuropsychology, 22,* 686–701.

Arnett, P.A., Rao, S.M., Grafman, J., Bernardin, L., Luchetta, T., Binder, J.R., & Lobeck, L. (1997). Executive functions in multiple sclerosis: An analysis of temporal ordering, semantic encoding, and planning abilities. *Neuropsychology, 11,* 535–544.

Atkinson, R.C., & Shiffrin, R.M. (1968). Human memory: A proposed system and its control processes. In K.W. Spence & J.T. Spence (Eds.), *The Psychology of learning and motivation* (Vol. 2). London: Academic Press.

Azouvi, P., Jokic, C., van der Linden, M., & Marlier, N. (1996). Working memory and supervisory control after severe closed-head injury: A study of dual task performance and random generation. *Journal of Clinical and Experimental Neuropsychology, 18,* 317–337.

Baddeley, A.D., Baddeley, H.A., Bucks, R.S., & Wilcock, G.K. (2001). Attentional control in Alzheimer's disease. *Brain, 124,* 1492–1508.

Baddeley, A.D., Chincotta, D., & Adlam, A. (2001). Working memory and the control of action: Evidence from task switching. *Journal of Experimental Psychology, General, 130,* 641–657.

Baddeley, A.D., Della Sala, S., Papagno, C., & Spinnler, H. (1997). Dual-task performance in dysexecutive and nondysexecutive patients with a frontal lesion. *Neuropsychology, 11,* 187–194.

Baddeley, A.D., & Hitch, G.J. (1974). Working memory. In G.H. Bower (Ed.), *The psychology of learning and motivation* (Vol. 8). London: Academic Press.

Bandstra, E.S., Morrow, C.E., Anthony, J.C., Accornero, V.H., & Fried, P.A.

(2001). Longitudinal investigation of task persistence and sustained attention in children with prenatal cocaine exposure. *Neurotoxicology and Teratology, 23*, 545–559.

Barkley, R.A. (1997). Behavioral inhibition, sustained attention and executive functions: Constructing a unifying theory of ADHD. *Psychological Bulletin, 121*, 65–94.

Barkley, R.A. (1999). Response inhibition in attention-deficit hyperactivity disorder. *Mental Retardation and Developmental Disabilities Research Reviews, 5*, 177–184.

Barkley, R.A., Edwards, G., Laneri, M., Fletcher, K., & Metevia, L. (2001). Executive functioning, temporal discounting, and sense of time in adolescents with attention deficit hyperactivity disorder (ADHD) and oppositional defiant disorder (ODD). *Journal of Abnormal Child Psychology, 29*, 541–556.

Barkley, R.A., Koplowitz, S., Anderson, T., & McMurray, M.B. (1997). Sense of time in children with ADHD: Effects of duration, distraction, and stimulant medication. *Journal of the International Neuropsychological Society, 3*, 359–369.

Barry, T.D., Klinger, L.G., Lyman, R.D., Bush, D., & Hawkins, L. (2001). Visual selective attention versus sustained attention in boys with attention-deficit/hyperactivity disorder. *Journal of Attention Disorders, 4*, 193–202.

Bate, A.J., Mathias, J.L., & Crawford, J.R. (2001). The covert orienting of visual attention following severe traumatic brain injury. *Journal of Clinical and Experimental Neuropsychology, 23*, 386–398.

Bayliss, D.M., & Roodenrys, S. (2000). Executive processing and attention deficit hyperactivity disorder: An application of the supervisory attentional system. *Developmental Neuropsychology, 17*, 161–180.

Bechtel, W. (1993). Currents in connectionism. *Minds and Machines, 3*, 125–153.

Benton, A.L. (1986). Reaction time in brain disease: Some reflections. *Cortex, 22*, 129–140.

Beschin, N., Cocchini, G., Della Sala, S., & Logie, R.H. (1997). What the eyes perceive, the brain ignores: A case of pure unilateral representational neglect. *Cortex, 33*, 3–26.

Bilder, R.M., Goldman, R.S., Robinson, D., Reiter, G., Bell, L., Bates, J.A., Pappadopulos, E., Willson, D.F., Alvir, J.M.J., Woerner, M.G., Geisler, S., Kane, J.M., & Lieberman, J.A. (2000). Neuropsychology of first-episode schizophrenia: Initial characterization and clinical correlates. *American Journal of Psychiatry, 157*, 549–559.

Bisiach, E., & Luzzati, C. (1978). Unilateral neglect of representational space. *Cortex, 14,* 129–133.

Botella, J., Contreras, M.J., Shih, P., & Rubio, V. (2001). Two short tests fail to detect vigilance decrements. *European Journal of Psychological Assessment, 17,* 48–55.

Bourke, P.A. (1997). Measuring attentional demand in continuous dual-task performance. *Quarterly Journal of Experimental Psychology: Human Experimental Psychology, 50A,* 821–840.

Bourke, P.A., Duncan, J., & Nimmo-Smith, I. (1996). A general factor involved in dual task performance decrement. *Quarterly Journal of Experimental Psychology, 49A,* 525–545.

Brebion, G., Smith, M.J., Gorman, J.M., & Amador, X. (1996). Reality monitoring failure in schizophrenia: The role of selective attention. *Schizophrenia Research, 22,* 173–180.

Broadbent, D.E. (1958). *Perception and communication.* Oxford, Pergamon.

Cherry, E.C. (1953). Some experiments on the recognition of speech with one and two ears. *Journal of the Acoustical Society of America, 25,* 975–979.

Bronowski, J. (1977). Human and animal language. In J. Bronowski (Ed.), *A sense of the future.* Cambridge, MA: MIT Press.

Brouwer, W.H., Ponds, R.W., van Wolffelaar, P.C., & van Zomeren, A.H. (1989). Divided attention 5 to 10 years after severe closed head injury. *Cortex, 25,* 219–230.

Brouwer, W.H., Withaar, F.K., Tant, M.L.M., & van Zomeren, A.H. (2002). Attention and driving in traumatic brain injury: A question of coping with time-pressure. *Journal of Head Trauma Rehabilitation, 17,* 1–15.

Brugger, P., Monsch, A.U., Salmon, D.P., & Butters, N. (1996). Random number generation in dementia of the Alzheimer type: A test of frontal executive functions. *Neuropsychologia, 34,* 97–103.

Bruins, R., & Nieuwenhuizen, C.H. (1990). PASAT is PVSAT? Projectverslag, internal report. Department of Neuropsychology, State University Groningen.

Bryson, G., Whelahan, H.A., & Bell, M. (2001). Memory and executive function impairments in deficit syndrome schizophrenia. *Psychiatry Research, 102,* 29–37.

Buchanan, R.W., Strauss, M.E., Kirkpatrick, B., & Holstein, C. (1994). Neuropsychological impairments in deficit vs nondeficit forms of schizophrenia. *Archives of General Psychiatry, 51,* 804–811.

Burgess, P.W., Alderman, N., Evans, J., Emslie, H., & Wilson, B.A. (1998).

The ecological validity of tests of executive function. *Journal of the International Neuropsychological Society, 4,* 547–558.

Bustini, M., Stratta, P., Daneluzzo, E., Pollice, R., Prosperini, P., & Rossi, A. (1999). Tower of Hanoi and WCST performance in schizophrenia: Problem-solving capacity and clinical correlates. *Journal of Psychiatric Research, 33,* 285–290.

Caffarra, P., Riggio, L., Malvezzi, L., Scaglioni, A., & Freedman, M. (1997). Orienting of visual attention in Alzheimer's disease: Its implication in favor of the interhemispheric balance. *Neuropsychiatry, Neuropsychology, and Behavioral Neurology, 10,* 90–95.

Calderon, J., Perry, R.J., Erzinclioglu, S.W., Berrios, G.E., Dening, T.R., & Hodges, J.R. (2001). Perception, attention, and working memory are disproportionately impaired in dementia with Lewy bodies compared with Alzheimer's disease. *Journal of Neurology, Neurosurgery and Psychiatry, 70,* 157–164.

Camicioli, R., Howieson, D., Lehman, S., & Kaye, J. (1997). Talking while walking: The effect of a dual task in aging and Alzheimer's disease. *Neurology, 48,* 955–958.

Carter, C.S., Robertson, L.C., Chaderjian, M.R., & Celaya, L.J. (1992). Attentional asymmetry in schizophrenia: Controlled and automated processes. *Biological Psychiatry, 31,* 909–918.

Carter, C.S., Robertson, L.C., Nordahl, T.E., & Chaderjian, M. (1996). Perceptual and attentional asymmetries in schizophrenia: Further evidence for a left hemisphere deficit. *Psychiatry Research, 62,* 111–119.

Cepeda, N.J., Cepeda, M.L., & Kramer, A.F. (2000). Task switching and attention deficit hyperactivity disorder. *Journal of Abnormal Child Psychology, 28,* 213–226.

Chen, S.T., Sultzer, D.L., Hinkin, C.H., Mahler, M.E., & Cummings, J.L. (1998). *Journal of Neuropsychiatry and Clinical Neurosciences, 10,* 426–432.

Christ, S.E., White, D.A., Brunstrom, J.E., & Abrams, R.A., (2003). Inhibitory control following perinatal brain injury. *Neuropsychology, 17,* 171–178.

Clark, L., Iversen, S.D., & Goodwin, G.M. (2002). Sustained attention deficit in bipolar disorder. *British Journal of Psychiatry, 180,* 313–319.

Clark, C., Prior, M., & Kinsella, G.J. (2000). Do executive function deficits differentiate between adolescents with ADHD and oppositional defiant/conduct disorder? A neuropsychological study using the Six Elements test and Hayling Sentence Completion test. *Journal of Abnormal Child Psychology, 28,* 403–414.

Cohen, R.M., Nordahl, T.E., Semple, W.E., Andreason, P., & Pickar, D. (1998). Abnormalities in the distributed network of sustained attention predict neuroleptic treatment response in schizophrenia. *Neuropsychopharmacology*, *19*, 36–47.

Collette, F., van der Linden, M., Bechet, S., Belleville, S., & Salmon, E. (1998). Working memory deficits in Alzheimer's disease. *Brain and Cognition*, *37*, 147–149.

Collins, L.F., & Long, C.J. (1996). Visual reaction time and its relationship to neuropsychological test performance. *Archives of Clinical Neuropsychology*, *11*, 613–623.

Comerford, V.E., Geffen, G.M., May, C., Medland, S.E., & Geffen, L.B. (2002). A rapid screen of the severity of mild traumatic brain injury. *Journal of Clinical and Experimental Neuropsychology*, *24*, 409–419.

Corteen, R.S., & Dunn, D. (1971). Shock associated words in a non-attended message: A test for momentary awareness. *Journal of Experimental Psychology*, *102*, 1143–1144.

Coslett, H.B., Stark, M., Rajaram, S., & Saffran, E.M. (1995). Narrowing the spotlight: A visual attentional disorder in presumed Alzheimer's disease. *Neurocase*, *1*, 305–318.

Cosway, R., Byrne, M., Clafferty, R., Hodges, A., Grant, E., Abukmeil, S.S., Lawrie, S.M., Miller, P., & Johnstone, E.C. (2000). Neuropsychological change in young people at high risk for schizophrenia: Results from the first two neuropsychological assessments of the Edinburgh High Risk Study. *Psychological Medicine*, *30*, 1111–1121.

Cosway, R., Byrne, M., Clafferty, R., Hodges, A., Grant, E., Morris, J., Abukmeil, S.S., Lawrie, S.M., Miller, P., Cowens, D.G.C., & Johnstone, E.C. (2002). Sustained attention in young people at high risk for schizophrenia. *Psychological Medicine*, *32*, 277–286.

Coull, J.T., Frith, C.D., Frackowiak, R.S.J., & Grasby, P.M. (1996). A frontoparietal network for rapid visual information processing: A PET study of sustained attention and working memory. *Neuropsychologia*, *34*, 1085–1095.

Craik, F.I.M., & Lockhart, R.S. (1972). Levels of processing: A framework for memory research. *Journal of Verbal Learning and Verbal Behaviour*, *11*, 671–684.

Crawford, J.R., Bryan, J., Luszcz, M.A., Obonsawin, M.C., & Stewart, L. (2000). The executive decline hypothesis of cognitive aging: Do executive deficits qualify as differential deficits and do they mediate age-related memory decline? *Aging, Neuropsychology and Cognition*, *7*, 9–31.

Crook, T.H., West, R.L., & Larrabee, G.J. (1993). The driving-reaction time test: Assessing age declines in dual-task performance. *Developmental Neuropsychology, 9,* 31–39.

Culbertson, W.C., & Zillmer, E.A. (1998). The construct validity of the Tower of London-super(DX) as a measure of the executive functioning of ADHD children. *Assessment, 5,* 215–226.

Dehaene, S., & Changeux, J.P. (1991). The Wisconsin Card Sorting test: Theoretical analysis and modelling in a neural network. *Cerebral Cortex, 1,* 62–79.

Demakis, G.J., (2003). A meta-analytic review of the sensitivity of the Wisconsin Card Sorting task to frontal and lateralized frontal brain damage. *Neuropsychology, 17,* 255–264.

Demaree, H.A., DeLuca, J., Gaudino, E.A., & Diamond, B.J. (1999). Speed of information processing as a key deficit in multiple sclerosis: Implications for rehabilitation. *Journal of Neurology, Neurosurgery and Psychiatry, 67,* 661–663.

D'Erme, P., Robertson, I., Bartolomeo, P., & Daniele, A. (1992). Early rightwards orienting of attention on simple reaction time performance in patients with left-sided neglect. *Neuropsychologia, 30,* 989–1000.

D'Esposito, M., Detre, J.A., Alsop, D.C., Shin, R.K., Atlas, S., & Grossman, M. (1995). The neural basis of the central executive system of working memory. *Nature, 378,* 279–281.

D'Esposito, M., Onishi, K., Thompson, H., Robinson, K., Armstrong, C., & Grossman, M. (1996). Working memory impairments in multiple sclerosis: Evidence from a dual-task paradigm. *Neuropsychology, 10,* 51–56.

Detweiler, M.C., & Lundy, D.H. (1995). Effects of single- and dual-task practice on acquiring dual-task skills. *Human Factors, 37,* 193–211.

Deutsch, J.A., & Deutsch, D. (1963). Attention: Some theoretical considerations. *Psychological Review, 93,* 283–321.

Dickinson, D., & Coursey, R.D. (2002). Independence and overlap among neurocognitive correlates of community functioning in schizophrenia. *Schizophrenia Research, 56,* 161–170.

Dinn, W.M., Robbins, N.C., & Harris, C.L. (2001). Adult attention-deficit/ hyperactivity disorder: Neuropsychological correlates and clinical presentation. *Brain and Cognition, 46,* 114–121.

Driesen, N.R., Cox, D.J., Gonder-Frederick, L., & Clarke, W. (1995). Reaction time impairment in insulin-dependent diabetes: Task complexity, blood glucose levels, and individual differences. *Neuropsychology, 9,* 246–254.

Driver, J. (2001). A selective review of selective attention research from the past century. *British Journal of Psychology, 92,* 53–78.

REFERENCES

Duchek, J.M., Hunt, L., Ball, K., & Buckles, V. (1997). The role of selective attention in driving and dementia of the Alzheimer type. *Alzheimer Disease and Associated Disorders, 11(Suppl 1)*, 48–56.

Duke, L.M., & Kaszniak, A.W. (2000). Executive control functions in degenerative dementias: A comparative review. *Neuropsychology Review, 10*, 75–99.

Duncan, J. (1996). Coordinated brain systems in selective perception and action. In T. Innui & J.L. McClelland (Eds.), *Attention and performance, XVI*, (pp. 549–578). Cambridge, MA: MIT Press.

Duncan, J., Burgess, P., & Emslie, H. (1995). Fluid intelligence after frontal lobe lesions. *Neuropsychologia, 33*, 261–268.

Duncan, J., Emslie, H., Williams, P., Johnson, R., & Freer, C. (1996). Intelligence and the frontal lobe: The organization of goal-directed behaviour. *Cognitive Psychology, 30*, 257–303.

Duncan, J., Johnson, R., Swales, M., & Freer, C. (1997). Frontal lobe deficits after head injury: Unity and diversity of function. *Cognitive Neuropsychology, 14*, 713–741.

Duncan, J., Seitz, R., Kolodny, J., Bor, D., Herzog, H., Ahmed, A., Newell, F., & Emslie, H. (2000). A neural basis for general intelligence. *Science, 289*, 457–460.

Ellis, A.W., & Young, A.W. (1988). *Human cognitive neuropsychology*. Hove, UK: Psychology Press.

Evans, J.J., Chua, S.E., McKenna, P.J., & Wilson, B.A. (1997). Assessment of the dysexecutive syndrome in schizophrenia. *Psychological Medicine, 27*, 635–646.

Faraone, S.V., & Biederman, J. (1998). Neurobiology of attention-deficit hyperactivity disorder. *Biological Psychiatry, 44*, 951–958.

Fink, G.R., Halligan, P.W., Marshall, J.C., Frith, C.D., Frackowiak, R.S.J., & Dolan, R.J. (1996). Where in the brain does visual attention select the forest and the trees? *Nature, 382*, 626–628.

Fisk, J.E., & Warr, P. (1996). Age and working memory: The role of perceptual speed, the central executive and the phonological loop. *Psychology and Aging, 11*, 316–323.

Flashman, L.A., Horner, M.D., & Freides, D. (1991). Note on scoring perseveration on the Wisconsin Card Sorting test. *The Clinical Neuropsychologist, 5*, 190–194.

Fleck, D.E., Shear, P.K., & Strakowski, S.M. (2002). A reevaluation of sustained attention performance in temporal lobe epilepsy. *Archives of Clinical Neuropsychology, 17*, 399–405.

Fuster, J.M. (1989). *The prefrontal cortex*. New York: Raven Press.

Gainotti, G., Marra, CA., & Villa, G., (2001). A double dissociation between accuracy and time of execution on attentional tasks in Alzheimer's disease and multi-infarct dementia. *Brain, 124,* 731–738.

Gansler, D.A., Fucetola, R., Krengel, M., Stetson, S., Zimering, R., & Makary, C. (1998). Are there cognitive subtypes in adult attention deficit/ hyperactivity disorder? *Journal of Nervous and Mental Disease, 186,* 776–781.

Gehring, W.J., & Knight, R.T. (2002). Lateral prefrontal damage affects processing selection but not attention switching. *Cognitive Brain Research, 13,* 267–279.

Giambra, L.M., & Quilter, R.E. (1988). Sustained attention in adulthood: A unique, large-sample, longitudinal and multicohort analysis using the Mackworth Clock Test. *Psychology and Aging, 3,* 75–83.

Gilbert, S.J., & Shallice, T. (2002). Task switching: A PDP model. *Cognitive Psychology, 44,* 297–337.

Giovannetti, T., Goldstein, R.Z., Schullery, M., Barr, W.B., & Bilder, R.M. (2003). Category fluency in first episode schizophrenia. *Journal of the International Neuropsychological Society, 9,* 384–393.

Goldman, R.S., Axelrod, B.N., Tandon, R., & Berent, S. (1991). Analysis of executive functioning in schizophrenics using the Wisconsin Card Sorting test. *Journal of Nervous and Mental Disease, 179,* 507–508.

Goldman-Rakic, P.S. (1995). Anatomical and functional circuits in prefrontal cortex of nonhuman primates: Relevance to epilepsy. In H.H. Jasper, S. Riggio, & P.S. Goldman-Rakic (Eds.), *Epilepsy and the functional anatomy of the frontal lobe* (pp. 51–62). New York: Raven Press.

Gordon, W.A., & Diller, L. (1983). Stroke: Coping with a cognitive deficit. In T.E. Burish & L.A. Bradley (Eds.), *Coping with chronic disease.* San Diego, CA: Academic Press.

Grande, L., McGlinchey-Berroth, R., Milberg, W.P., & D'Esposito, M. (1996). Facilitation of unattended semantic information in Alzheimer's disease: Evidence from a selective attention task. *Neuropsychology, 10,* 475–484.

Graw, P., Werth, E., Kraeuchi, K., Gutzwiller, F., Cajochen, C., & Wirz-Justice, A., (2001). Early morning melatonin administration impairs psychomotor vigilance. *European Journal of Psychological Assessment, 17,* 48–55.

Greene, J.D.W., Hodges, J.R., & Baddeley, A.D. (1995). Autobiographical memory and executive function in early dementia of Alzheimer type. *Neuropsychologia, 33,* 1647–1670.

Gregory, C., Lough, S., Stone, V., Erzinclioglu, S., Martin, L., Baron-Cohen,

REFERENCES

S., & Hodges, J.R. (2002). Theory of mind in patients with frontal variant frontotemporal dementia and Alzheimer's disease: Theoretical and practical implications. *Brain, 125,* 752–764.

Grodzinsky, G.M., & Barkley, R.A. (1999). Predictive power of frontal lobe tests in the diagnosis of attention-deficit hyperactivity disorder. *Clinical Neuropsychologist, 13,* 12–21.

Gronwall, D. (1977). Paced Auditory Serial Addition task: A measure of recovery from concussion. *Perceptual and Motor Skills, 44,* 367–373.

Gronwall, D., & Wrightson P. (1974). Delayed recovery of intellectual function after minor head injury. *Lancet, 2,* 995–997.

Hale, T.S., Hariri, A.R., & McCracken, J.T. (2000). Attention-deficit/ hyperactivity disorder: Perspectives from neuroimaging. *Mental Retardation and Developmental Disabilities Research Reviews, 6,* 214–219.

Halligan, P.W., Manning, L., & Marshall, J.C. (1991). Hemispheric activation vs. spatio-motor cueing in visual neglect: A single case study. *Neuropsychologia, 29,* 165–176.

Halligan, P.W., Marshall, J.C., & Wade, D.T. (1990). Do visual field deficits exacerbate visuo-spatial neglect? *Journal of Neurology, Neurosurgery and Psychiatry, 53,* 487–491.

Harmer, C.J., Clark, L., & Grayson, L., & Goodwin, G.M. (2002). Sustained attention deficit in bipolar disorder is not a working memory impairment in disguise. *Neuropsychologia, 40,* 1586–1590.

Hart, S., & Semple, J.M. (1990). *Neuropsychology and the dementias.* Philadelphia, PA: Taylor and Francis.

Hart, R.P., Wade, J.B., Klinger, R.L., & Hamer, R.M. (1990). Slowed information processing as an early cognitive change associated with HIV infection. *Neuropsychology, 4,* 97–104.

Heilman, K.M., & Valenstein, E. (1979). Mechanisms underlying hemispatial neglect. *Annals of Neurology, 5,* 166–170.

Heinze, H.J., Mangun, G.R., Burchert, W., & Hinrichs, H. (1994). Combined spatial and temporal imaging of brain activity during visual selective attention in humans. *Nature, 372,* 543–546.

Henderson, L., & Dittrich, W.H. (1998). Preparing to react in the absence of uncertainty: I. New perspectives on simple reaction time. *British Journal of Psychology, 89,* 531–554.

Herath, P., Klingberg, T., Young, J., Amunts, K., & Roland, P. (2001). Neural correlates of dual task interference can be dissociated from those of divided attention: An fMRI study. *Cerebral Cortex, 11,* 796–805.

Hill, S.K., Gur, R.C., & Gur, R.E. (2001). Neuropsychological differences among empirically derived clinical subtypes of schizophrenia. *Neuropsychology, 15,* 492–501.

Hill, D.E., Yeo, R.A., Campbell, R.A., Hart, B., Vigil, J., & Brooks, W. (2003). Magnetic resonance imaging correlates of attention deficit/hyperactivity disorder in children. *Neuropsychology, 17,* 496–506.

Hillyard, S.A., Hinrichs, H., Tempelmann, C., Morgan, S.T., Hansen, J.C., Scheich, H., & Heinze, H.-J. (1997). Combining steady-state visual evoked potentials and fMRI to localize brain activity during selective attention. *Human Brain Mapping, 5,* 287–292.

Hinton-Bayre, A.D., Geffen, G., & McFarland, K. (1997). Mild head injury and speed of information processing: A prospective study of professional rugby league players. *Journal of Clinical & Experimental Neuropsychology, 19,* 275–289.

Hjaltason, H., Tegner, R., Tham, K., & Levander, M. (1996). Sustained attention and awareness of disability in chronic neglect. *Neuropsychologia, 34,* 1229–1233.

Hooks, K., Milich, R., & Lorch, E.P. (1994). Sustained and selective attention in boys with attention deficit hyperactivity disorder. *Journal of Clinical Child Psychology, 23,* 69–77.

Holst, P., & Vilkki, J. (1988). Effect of frontal medial lesions on performance on the Stroop test and word fluency tasks. *Journal of Experimental and Clinical Neuropsychology, 10,* 79–80.

Houghton, S., Douglas, G., West, J., Whiting, K., Wall, M., Langsford, S., Powell, L., & Carroll, A. (1999). Differential patterns of executiive function in children with attention-deficit hyperactivity disorder according to gender and subtype. *Journal of Child Neurology, 14,* 801–805.

Hubel, D.H., & Wiesel, T.N. (1979). Brain mechanisms of vision. *Scientific American, 249,* 150–162.

Humphreys, G.W., & Riddoch, M.J. (1992). Interactions between object- and space-vision revealed through neuropsychology. In D.E. Meyer & S. Kornblum (Eds.), *Attention and performance XIV,* Hillsdale, NJ: Lawrence Erlbaum Associates, Inc.

Humphreys, G.W., & Riddoch, M.J. (1993). Interactive attentional systems and unilateral visual neglect. In I.H. Robertson & J.C. Marshall, (Eds.), *Unilateral neglect: Clinical and experimental studies.* Hove, UK: Lawrence Erlbaum Associates Ltd.

Hutton, S.B., Puri, B.K., Duncan, L.-J., Robbins, T.W., Barnes, T.R.E., & James, W. (1890). *Principles of Psychology.* New York: Holt.

Joyce, E.M. (1998). Executive function in first-episode schizophrenia. *Psychological Medicine, 28*, 463–473.

Hynd, G.W., Nieves, N, Connor, R.T., & Stone, P. (1989). Attention deficit disorder with and without hyperactivity: Reaction time and speed of cognitive processing. *Journal of Learning Disabilities, 22*, 573–580.

Ihara, H., Berrios, G.E., & McKenna, P.J. (2000). Dysexecutive syndrome in schizophrenia: A cross-cultural comparison between Japanese and British patients. *Behavioural Neurology, 12*, 209–220.

Iwanami, A., Isono, H., Okajima, Y., Noda, Y., & Kamijima, K. (1998). Event-related potentials during a selective attention task with short inter-stimulus intervals in patients with schizophrenia. *Journal of Psychiatry & Neuroscience, 23*, 45–50.

Iversen, S.D., & Dunnett, S.B. (1990). Functional organization of striatum as studied with neural grafts. *Neuropsychologia, 28*, 601–626.

Johnston, B, Hogg, J.R., Schopp, L.H., Kapila, C., & Edwards, S. (2002). Neuropsychological deficit profiles in senile dementia of the Alzheimer's type. *Archives of Clinical Neuropsychology, 17*, 273–281.

Jones, L.A., Cardno, A.G., Sanders, R.D., Owen, M.J., & Williams, J. (2001). Sustained and selective attention as measures of genetic liability to schizophrenia. *Schizophrenia Research, 48*, 263–272.

Jonkman, L.M., Kemner, C., Verbaten, M.N., & Koelega, H.S. (1997). Event-related potentials and performance of attention-deficit hyperactivity disorder: Children and normal controls in auditory and visual selective attention tasks. *Biological Psychiatry, 41*, 595–611.

Kass, S.J., Vodanovich, S.J., Stanny, C.J., & Taylor, T.M. (2001). Watching the clock: Boredom and vigilance performance. *Perceptual and Motor Skills, 92*, 969–976.

Keller, I., Schlenker, A., & Pigache, R.M. (1995). Selective impairment of auditory attention following closed head injuries or right cerebrovascular accidents. *Cognitive Brain Research, 3*, 9–15.

Kempton, S., Vance, A., Maruff, P., Luk, E., Costin, J., & Pantelis, C. (1999). Executive function and attention deficit hyperactivity disorder: Stimulant medication and better executive function performance in children. *Psychological Medicine, 29*, 527–538.

Kenny, J.T., Friedman, L., Findling, R.L., Swales, T.P., Strauss, M.E., Jesberger, J.A., & Schulz, S.C. (1997). Cognitive impairment in adolescents with schizophrenia. *American Journal of Psychiatry, 154*, 1613–1615.

Kim, M.S., & Robertson, L.C. (2001). Implicit representations of space after bilateral parietal lobe damage. *Journal of Cognitive Neuroscience, 13*, 1080–1087.

Knights, R.T., Grabowecky, M.F., & Scabini, D. (1995). Role of human pre-frontal cortex in attention control. In H.H. Jasper, S. Riggio, & P.S. Goldman-Rakic (Eds.), *Epilepsy and the functional anatomy of the frontal lobe*. New York: Raven Press.

Kramer, J.H., Reed, B.R., Mungas, D., Weiner, M.W., & Chui, H.C. (2002). Executive dysfunction in subcortical ischaemic vascular disease. *Journal of Neurology, Neurosurgery and Psychiatry, 72*, 217–220.

Kremen, W.S., Seidman, L.J., Faraone, S.V., & Tsuang, M.T. (2003). Is there disproportionate impairment in semantic or phonemic fluency in schizophrenia. *Journal of the International Neuropsychological Society, 9*, 79–88.

Ladavas, E. (1990). Selective spatial attention in patients with visual extinction. *Brain, 113*, 1527–1538.

Langley, L.K., Overmier, J.B., Knopman, D.S., & Prod'Homme, M.M. (1998). Inhibition and habituation: Preserved mechanisms of attentional selection in aging and Alzheimer's disease. *Neuropsychology, 12*, 353–366.

Laws, K.R., McKenna, P.J., & McCarthy, R.A. (1999). Reconsidering the gospel according to group studies: A neuropsychological case study approach to schizophrenia. *Cognitive Neuropsychiatry, 1*, 319–343.

Lenzenweger, M.F., Cornblatt, B.A., & Putnick, M. (1991). Schizotypy and sustained attention. *Journal of Abnormal Psychology, 100*, 84–89.

Le, Tuong H., Pardo, J.V., & Hu, X. (1998). 4T-fMRI study of nonspatial shifting of selective attention: Cerebellar and parietal contributions. *Journal of Neurophysiology, 79*, 1535–1548.

Levin, H.S., Fletcher, J.M., Kufera, J.A., & Harward, H. (1996). Dimensions of cognition measured by the Tower of London and other cognitive tasks in head-injured children and adolescents. *Developmental Neuropsychology, 12*, 17–34.

Lezak, M.D. (1983). *Neuropsychological assessment*. New York: Oxford University Press.

Litvan, I., Mohr, E., Williams, J., & Gomez, C. (1991). Differential memory and executive functions in demented patients with Parkinson's and Alzheimer's disease. *Journal of Neurology, Neurosurgery and Psychiatry, 54*, 25–29.

Lockwood, K.A., Marcotte, A.C., & Stern, C. (2001). Differentiation of attention-deficit/hyperactivity disorder subtypes: Application of neuropsychological model of attention. *Journal of Clinical and Experimental Neuropsychology, 23*, 317–330.

REFERENCES

Loken, W., Thornton, A.E., Otto, R.L., & Long, C.J. (1995). Sustained attention after severe closed head injury. *Neuropsychology, 9,* 592–598.

Lough, S., Gregory, C., & Hodges, J.R. (2001). Dissociation of social cognition and executive function in frontal variant frontotemporal dementia. *Neurocase, 7,* 123–130.

Luck, S.J. (1998). Sources of dual-task interference: Evidence from human electrophysiology. *Psychological Science, 9,* 223–227.

Lussier, I., & Stip, E. (1999). Attention selective et schizophrenie avant l'administration de neuroleptiques. [Selective attention in never-medicated patients with schizophrenia]. *Encephale, 25,* 576–583.

Mack, J.L., & Patterson, M.B. (1995). Executive dysfunction and Alzheimer's disease: Performance on a test of planning ability, the Porteus Maze test. *Neuropsychology, 9,* 556–564.

Macmillan, M. (2000). Restoring Phineas Gage: A 150th retrospective. *Journal of the History of the Neurosciences, 9,* 46–66.

Mackworth, N.H. (1950). Researches in the measurement of human performance. MRC special report no. 268. In H.A. Sinaiko (Ed.), 1961, *Selected papers on human factors in the design and use of control systems.* London: Dover.

Maddox, W.T., Filoteo, J.V., Delis, D.C., & Salmon, D.P. (1996). Visual selective attention deficits in patients with Parkinson's disease: A quantitative model-based approach. *Neuropsychology, 10,* 197–218.

Mahone, E.M., Koth, C.W., Cutting, L., Singer, H.S., & Denckla, M.B. (2001). Executive function in fluency and recall measures among children with Tourette syndrome or ADHD. *Journal of the International Neuropsychological, 7,* 102–111.

Mangun, G.R., Hopfinger, J.B., Kussmaul, C.L., Fletcher, E.M., & Heinze, H-J. (1997). Covariations in ERP and PET measures of spatial selective attention in human extrastriate visual cortex. *Human Brain Mapping, 5,* 273–279.

Manly, T., Anderson, V., Nimmo-Smith, I., Turner, A., Watson, P., & Robertson, I.H. (2001). The differential assessment of children's attention: The Test of Everyday Attention for Children (TEA-Ch), normative sample and ADHD performance. *Journal of Child Psychology and Psychiatry and Allied Disciplines, 42,* 1065–1081.

Manly, T., Robertson, I.H., Anderson, V., & Nimmo-Smith, I. (1998). *The Test of Everyday Attention for Children (TEA-Ch).* Bury St Edmunds, UK: Thames Valley Test Publishing Company.

Mar, C.M., Smith, D.A., & Sarter, M. (1996). Behavioural vigilance in schizophrenia: Evidence for hyperattentional processing. *British Journal of Psychiatry, 169*, 781–789.

Marczewski, P., van der Linden, M., & Laroi, F. (2001). Further investigation of the supervisory attentional system in schizophrenia: Planning, inhibition, and rule abstraction. *Cognitive Neuropsychiatry, 6*, 175–192.

Marr, D. (1982). *Vision: A computation investigation into the human representation and processing of visual information.* San Francisco, CA: W.H. Freeman.

McCloskey, M. (1991). Networks and theories: The place of connectionism in cognitive science. *Psychological Science, 2*, 387–395.

McGrath, J., Scheldt, S., Hengtsberger, P., & Dark, F. (1997). Thought disorder and executive ability. *Cognitive Neuropsychiatry, 2*, 303–314.

McKeith, I., Fairbairn, A., Briel, R., & Harrison, R. (1993). Lewy bodies and Alzheimer's disease. *British Journal of Psychiatry, 163*, 262–263.

Mecklinger, A., von Cramon, D.Y., Springer, A., & Matthes-von Cramon, G. (1999). Executive control functions in task switching: Evidence from brain injured patients. *Journal of Clinical and Experimental Neuropsychology, 21*, 606–619.

Michiels, V., de Gucht, V., Cluydts, R., & Fischler, B. (1999). Attention and information processing efficiency in patients with chronic fatigue syndrome. *Journal of Clinical and Experimental Neuropsychology, 21*, 709–729.

Milner, B. (1963). Effects of different brain lesions on card sorting. *Archives of Neurology, 9*, 90–100.

Milner, B. (1995). Aspects of human frontal lobe function. In H.H. Jasper, S. Riggio, & P.S. Goldman-Rakic (Eds.), *Epilepsy and the functional anatomy of the frontal lobe.* New York: Raven Press.

Minsky, M., & Papert, S. (1988). *Perceptrons* (2nd ed.). Cambridge, MA: MIT Press.

Moran, J., & Desimone, R. (1985). Selective attention gates visual processing in the extrastriate cortex. *Nature, 332*, 151–155.

Moray, N. (1959). Attention in dichotic listening: Affective cues and the influence of instructions. *Quarterly Journal of Experimental Psychology, 11*, 56–60.

Moray, N. (1969). *Listening and attention.* Oxford: Penguin Books.

Morice, R., & Delahunty, A. (1996). Frontal/executive impairments in schizophrenia. *Schizophrenia Bulletin, 22*, 125–137.

Myerson, J., Lawrence, B., Hale, S., Jenkins, L., & Chen, J. (1998). General slowing of lexical and nonlexical information processing in dementia of the Alzheimer type. *Aging, Neuropsychology, and Cognition*, *5*, 182–193.

Myles-Worsley, M., Coon, H., & Byerley, W. (1998). The sensitivity of the Spontaneous Selective Attention test (SSAT): A study of schizophrenic inpatients and outpatients versus normal controls. *Schizophrenia Research*, *31*, 131–139.

Nash, A.J., & Fernandez, M. (1996). P300 and allocation of attention in dual-tasks. *International Journal of Psychophysiology*, *23*, 171–180.

Nathan, J., Wilkinson, D., Stammers, S., & Low, J.L. (2001). The role of tests of frontal executive function in the detection of mild dementia. *International Journal of Geriatric Psychiatry*, *16*, 18–26.

Nelson, H.E. (1976). A modified card sorting test sensitive to frontal lobe deficits. *Cortex*, *12*, 313–324.

Nestor, P.G., Faux, S.F., McCarley, R.W., & Penhune, V. (1992). Attentional cues in chronic schizophrenia: Abnormal disengagement of attention. *Journal of Abnormal Psychology*, *101*, 682–689.

Nigg, J.T. (2001). Is ADHD a disinhibitory disorder? *Psychological Bulletin*, *127*, 571–598.

Nigg, J.T., Butler, K.M., Huang-Pollock, C.L., & Henderson, J.M. (2002). Inhibitory processes in adults with persistent childhood onset ADHD. *Journal of Consulting and Clinical Psychology*, *70*, 153–157.

Norris, G., & Tate, R.L. (2000). The Behavioural Assessment of the Dysexecutive Syndrome (BADS): Ecological, concurrent and construct validity. *Neuropsychological Rehabilitation*, *10*, 33–45.

Oie, M., Rund, B.R., & Sundet, K. (1998a). Covert visual attention in patients with early-onset schizophrenia. *Schizophrenia Research*, *34*, 195–205.

Oie, M., Rund, B.R., Sundet, K., & Bryhn, G. (1998b). Auditory laterality and selective attention: Normal performance in patients with early-onset schizophrenia. *Schizophrenia Bulletin*, *24*, 643–652.

Okazaki, S., Kawakubo, Y., Hosokawa, M., & Maekawa, H. (2001). Response execution and/or inhibition in children with attention deficit/hyperactivity disorder during the Continuous Performance test. *Japanese Journal of Special Education*, *38*, 1–10.

Osterrieth, P.A. (1944). Le test de copie d'une figure complexe. *Archives de Psychologie*, *30*, 206–356.

Pandurangi, A.K., Sax, K.W., Pelonero, A.L., & Goldberg, S.C. (1994). Sustained attention and positive formal thought disorder in schizophrenia. *Schizophrenia Research*, *13*, 109–116.

Pantelis, C., Barnes, T.R.E., Nelson, H.E., Tanner, S., Weatherley, L.,Owen, A.M., & Robbins, T.W. (1997). Frontal–striatal cognitive deficits in patients with chronic schizophrenia. *Brain, 120,* 1823–1843.

Parasuraman, R., Greenwood, P.M., & Alexander, G.E. (1995). Selective impairment of spatial attention during visual search in Alzheimer's disease. *Neuroreport: An International Journal for the Rapid Communication of Research in Neuroscience, 6,* 1861–1864.

Parasuraman, R., Greenwood, P.M., & Alexander, G.E. (2000). Alzheimer's disease constricts the dynamic range of spatial attention in visual search. *Neuropsychologia, 38,* 1126–1135.

Parasuraman, R., & Haxby, J.V. (1993). Attention and brain function in Alzheimer's disease: A review. *Neuropsychology, 7,* 242–272.

Parasuraman, R., & Nestor, P.G. (1991). Attention and driving skills in aging and Alzheimer's disease. *Human Factors, 33,* 539–557.

Parker, D., & Crawford, J. (1992). Assessment of frontal lobe dysfunction. In J.R. Crawford, D.M. Parker, & W.W. McKinlay (Eds.), *A handbook of neuropsychological assessment.* Hove, UK: Lawrence Erlbaum Associates Ltd.

Pashler, H. (1994a). Dual-task interference in simple tasks: Data and theory. *Psychological Bulletin, 116,* 220–244.

Pashler, H. (1994b). Graded capacity-sharing in dual-task interference? *Journal of Experimental Psychology: Human Perception and Performance, 20,* 330–342.

Patterson, M.B., Mack, J.L., Geldmacher, D.S., & Whitehouse, P.J. (1996). Executive functions and Alzheimer's disease: Problems and prospects. *European Journal of Neurology, 3,* 5–15.

Pavese, A., Coslett, H.B., Saffran, E., & Buxbaum, L. (2002). Limitations of attentional orienting. Effects of abrupt visual onsets and offsets on naming two objects in a patient with simultanagnosia. *Neuropsychologia, 40,* 1097–1103.

Perchet, C., Revol, O., Fourneret, P., Mauguiere, F., & Garcia-Larrea, L. (2001). Attention shifts and anticipatory mechanics in hyperactive children: An ERP study using the Posner paradigm. *Biological Psychiatry, 50,* 44–57.

Perret, E. (1974). The left frontal lobe in man and the suppression of habitual responses in verbal categorical behaviour. *Neuropsychologia, 12,* 323–330.

Perry, R.J., Watson, P., & Hodges, J.R. (2000). The nature and staging of attention dysfunction in early (minimal and mild) Alzheimer's disease: Relationship to episodic and semantic memory impairment. *Neuropsychologia, 38,* 252–271.

Perugini, E.M., Harvey, E.A., Lovejoy, D.W., Sandstrom, K., & Webb, A.H. (2000). The predictive power of combined neuropsychological measures for attention-deficit/hyperactivity disorder in children. *Child Neuropsychology*, 6, 101–114.

Pigache, R.M. (1999). Vigilance in schizophrenia and its disruption by impaired preattentive selection: A dysintegration hypothesis. *Cognitive Neuropsychiatry*, 4, 119–144.

Plaut, D.C., & Shallice, T. (1993). Deep dyslexia: A case study of connectionist neuropsychology. *Cognitive Neuropsychology*, 10, 377–500.

Pollens, R.D., McBratnie, B.P., & Burton, P.L. (1988). Beyond cognition: Executive functions in closed head injury. *Cognitive Rehabilitation*, 6, 26–32.

Ponsford, J., & Kinsella, G. (1992). Attentional deficits following closed-head injury. *Journal of Clinical & Experimental Neuropsychology*, 14, 822–838.

Poole, J.H., Ober, B.A., Shenaut, G.K., & Vinogradov, S. (1999). Independent frontal-system deficits in schizophrenia: Cognitive, clinical, and adaptive implications. *Psychiatry Research*, 85, 161–176.

Poreh, A.M., Ross, T.P., & Whitman, R.D. (1995). Reexamination of executive functions in psychosis-prone college students. *Personality and Individual Differences*, 18, 535–539.

Posner, M.I. (1980). Orienting of attention. The VIIth Sir Frederick Bartlett lecture. *Quarterly Journal of Experimental Psychology*, 32A, 3–25.

Posner, M.I., & Peterson, S.E. (1990). The attention system of the human brain. *Annual Review of Neuroscience*, 13, 25–42.

Posner, M.I., Walker, J., Friedrich, F.J., & Rafal, R.D. (1984). Effects of parietal injury on covert orienting of attention. *Journal of Neuroscience*, 4, 1863–1874.

Rao, S.M., St Aubin-Faubert, P., & Leo, G.J. (1989). Information processing speed in patients with multiple sclerosis. *Journal of Clinical & Experimental Neuropsychology*, 11, 471–477.

Reitan, R.M. (1958). Validity of the Trailmaking test as an indication of organic brain damage. *Perceptual and Motor Skills*, 8, 271–276.

Rieger, M., Gauggel, S., & Burmeister, K., (2003). Inhibition of ongoing responses following frontal, non-frontal and basal ganglia lesions. *Neuropsychology*, 17, 272–282.

Robertson, I.H. (1993). The relationship between lateralized and non-lateralized attentional deficits in unilateral neglect. In D.E. Meyer & S. Kornblum (Eds.), *Attention and performance XIV*, Hillsdale, NJ: Lawrence Erlbaum Associates, Inc.

Robertson, I.H., Manly, T., Beschin, N., Daini, R., Haeske-Dewick, H., Hoemberg, V., Jehkonen, M., Pizzamiglio, G., Shiel, A., & Weber, E. (1997a). Auditory sustained attention is a marker of unilateral spatial neglect. *Neuropsychologia, 35*, 1527–1532.

Robertson, I.H., Ridgeway, V., Greenfield, E., & Parr, A. (1997b). Motor recovery after stroke depends on intact sustained attention: A 2-year follow-up study. *Neuropsychology, 11*, 290–295.

Robertson, I.H., Tegner, R., Tham, K., & Lo, A. (1995). Sustained attention training for unilateral neglect: Theoretical and rehabilitation implications. *Journal of Clinical & Experimental Neuropsychology, 17*, 416–430.

Robertson, I.H., Ward, T., Ridgeway, V., & Nimmo-Smith, I. (1994). *The Test of Everyday Attention*. Bury St Edmunds, UK: Thames Valley Test Publishing Company.

Robertson, I.H., Ward, T., Ridgeway, V., & Nimmo-Smith, I. (1996). Structure of normal human attention: The Test of Everyday Attention. *Journal of the International Neuropsychological Society, 2*, 525–534.

Rock, I., & Gutman, D. (1981). The effect of inattention on form perception. *Journal of Experimental Psychology, Human Perception and Performance, 7*, 275–285.

Rogers, W.A., Bertus, E.L., & Gilbert, D.K. (1994). Dual-task assessment of age differences in automatic process development. *Psychology and Aging, 9*, 398–413.

Rosvold, H.E., Mirsky, A.F., Sarason, I., Bransome, E.D., & Beck, L.H. (1956). A continuous performance test of brain damage. *Journal of Consulting Psychology, 20*, 343–350.

Royall, D.R., Cordes, J.A., & Polk, M. (1998). CLOX: An executive clock drawing task. *Journal of Neurology, Neurosurgery and Psychiatry, 64*, 588–594.

Rueckert, L., & Grafman, J. (1996). Sustained attention deficits in patients with right frontal lesions. *Neuropsychologia, 34*, 953–963.

Rumelhart, D.E., McClelland, J.L. and the PDP group (Eds.) (1986). *Parallel distributed processing: Vol. 1. Foundations*. Cambridge, MA: MIT Press.

Rumelhart, D.E, McClleland, J.L. and the PDP group (Eds.) (1986). *Parallel distributed processing: Vol. 2. Psychological and biological models*. Cambridge, MA: MIT Press.

Rund, B.R., Zeiner, P., Sundet, K., Oie, M., & Bryhn, G. (1998). No vigilance deficit found in either young schizophrenic or ADHD subjects. *Scandinavian Journal of Psychology, 39*, 101–107.

Ruthruff, E., Johnston, J.C., & Van Selst, M. (2001). Why practice reduces dual-task interference. *Journal of Experimental Psychology: Human Perception and Performance, 27*, 3–21.

Rypma, B., Berger, J., & D'Esposito, M. (2002). The influence of working memory demand and subject performance on prefrontal cortical activity. *Journal of Cognitive Neuroscience, 14*, 721–731.

Sahgal, A., Galloway, P.H., McKeith, I.G., & Edwardson, J.A. (1992). A comparative study of attentional deficits in senile dementias of Alzheimer and Lewy body types. *Dementia, 3*, 350–354.

Saoud, M., d'Amato, T., Gutknecht, C., Triboulet, P., Bertaud, J., Marie-Cardine, M., Dalery, J., & Rochet, T. (2000). Neuropsychological deficit in siblings discordant for schizophrenia. *Schizophrenia Bulletin, 26*, 893–902.

Sarter, M., Givens, B., & Bruno, J.P. (2001). The cognitive neuroscience of sustained attention: Where top-down meets bottom-up. *Brain Research Reviews, 35*, 146–160.

Shallice, T., (1988). *From neuropsychology to mental structure*. Cambridge University Press, Cambridge.

Schmitter-Edgecombe, M., & Kibby, M.K. (1998). Visual selective attention after severe closed head injury. *Journal of the International Neuropsychological Society, 4*, 144–159.

Schmitter-Edgecombe, M., & Roger, W.A. (1997). Automatic process development following severe closed head injury. *Neuropsychology, 11*, 296–308.

Schneider, S.J. (1976). Selective attention in schizophrenia. *Journal of Abnormal Psychology, 85*, 167–173.

Schreiber, H.E., Javorsky, D.J., Robinson, J.E., & Stern, R.A. (1999). Rey–Osterrieth Complex Figure performance in adults with attention deficit hyperactivity disorder: A validation study of the Boston Qualitative Scoring System. *Clinical Neuropsychologist, 13*, 509–520.

Schwartz, B.D., Livingston, J.E., Sautter, F., & Nelson, A. (1990). Sustained attention by schizophrenics. *New Trends in Experimental and Clinical Psychiatry, 6*, 169–176.

Schwartz, M.F., Mayer, N.H., FitzpatrickDeSalme, E.J., & Montgomery, M.W. (1993). Cognitive theory and the study of everyday action disorders after brain damage. *Journal of Head Trauma Rehabilitation, 8*, 59–72.

Semba, K. (2000). Multiple output pathways of the basal forebrain: Organization, chemical heterogeneity, and roles in vigilance. *Behavioural Brain Research, 115*, 117–141.

Shallice, T. (1982). Specific impairments in planning. *Philosophical Transactions of the Royal Society, London, [Biol]*, *298*, 199–209.

Shallice, T. (1988). *From neuropsychology to mental structure*. Cambridge: Cambridge University Press.

Shallice, T. (1991). From neuropsychology to mental structure. *Behavioural and Brain Sciences*, *14*, 429–439.

Shallice, T., & Warrington, E.K. (1970). Independent functioning of verbal memory stores: A neuropsychological study. *Quarterly Journal of Experimental Psychology*, *22*, 261–273.

Shiffrin, R.M., & Schneider, W. (1977). Controlled and automatic human information processing: II. Perceptual learning, automatic attending and a general theory. *Psychological Review*, *84*, 127–190.

Sieroff, E., & Urbanski M. (2002). Conditions of visual verbal extinction: Does the ipsilesional stimulus have to be identified? *Brain and Cognition*, *48*, 563–569.

Simone, P.M., & Baylis, G.C. (1997). Selective attention in a reaching task: Effect of normal aging and Alzheimer's disease. *Journal of Experimental Psychology: Human Perception and Performance*, *23*, 595–608.

Snyder, P.J., Capelleri, J.C., Archibald, C.J., & Fisk, J.D. (2001). Improved detection of differential information processing speed deficits between two disease course types of multiple sclerosis. *Neuropsychology*, *15*, 617–625.

Sperling, G. (1960). The information available in brief visual presentations. *Psychological Monograph*, *74*, 1–29.

Spikman, J.M., Deelman, B.G., & van Zomeren, A.H. (2000). Executive functioning, attention, and frontal lesions in patients with chronic CHI. *Journal of Clinical and Experimental Neuropsychology*, *22*, 325–338.

Stip, E., Lussier, I., Lalonde, P., Luyet, A., & Fabian, J. (1999). Neuroleptiques atypiques et attention selective. [Atypical neuroleptics and selective attention in schizophrenia]. *Encephale*, *25*, 260–264.

Stratta, P., Mancini, F., Mattei, P., Daneluzzo, E., Casacchia, M., & Rossi, A. (1997). Association between striatal reduction and poor Wisconsin Card Sorting test performance in patients with schizophrenia. *Biological Psychiatry*, *42*, 816–820.

Strayer, D., & Johnston, W.A. (2001). Driven to distraction: Dual-task studies of simulated driving and conversing on a cellular telephone. *Psychological Science*, *12*, 462–466.

Stroop, J.R. (1935). Studies of interference in serial verbal reactions. *Journal of Experimental*, *18*, 643–662.

REFERENCES

Stuss, D.T., & Gow, C.A. (1992). "Frontal dysfunction" after traumatic brain injury. *Neuropsychiatry, Neuropsychology, and Behavioral Neurology*, 5, 272–282.

Suhr, J.A. (1997). Executive functioning deficits in hypothetically psychosis-prone college students. *Schizophrenia Research*, 27, 29–35.

Taylor, S.F., Kornblum, S., & Tandon, R. (1996). Facilitation and interference of selective attention in schizophrenia. *Journal of Psychiatric Research*, 30, 251–259.

Thompson-Schill, S.L., Jonides, J., Marshietz, C., Smith, E.E., D'Esposito, M., Kan, I.P., Knight, R.T., & Swick, D. (2002). Effects of frontal lobe damage on interference effects in working memory. *Cognitive, Affective and Behavioural Neuroscience*, 2, 109–120.

Tipper, S.P. (1985). The negative priming effect: Inhibitory effects of ignored primes. *Quarterly Journal of Experimental Psychology*, 37A, 571–590.

Treisman, A.M. (1964). Verbal cues, language and meaning in selective attention. *Quarterly Journal of Experimental Psychology*, 40A, 201–237.

Treisman, A.M. (1960). Contextual cues in selective listening. *Quarterly Journal of Experimental Psychology*, 12, 242–248.

Treisman, A.M. (1988). Features and objects: The fourteenth Bartlett memorial lecture. *Quarterly Journal of Experimental Psychology*, 40A, 201–237.

Tsourtos, G., Thompson, J. C., & Stough, C. (2002). Evidence of an early information processing speed deficit in unipolar major depression. *Psychological Medicine*, 32, 259–265.

Ungerleider, L.G., & Mishkin, M. (1982). Two cortical visual systems. In D.J. Ingle, M.A. Goodale, & R.J.W. Mansfield (Eds.), *Analysis of visual behaviour*. Cambridge, MA: MIT Press.

van Zomeren, A.H., & Brouwer, W.H. (1992). Assessment of attention. In J.R. Crawford, D.M. Parker, & W.W. McKinlay (Eds.), *A handbook of neuropsychological assessment*. Hove, UK: Lawrence Erlbaum Associates Ltd.

van Zomeren, A.H., & Deelman, B.G. (1978). Long-term recovery of visual reaction time after closed head injury. *Journal of Neurology, Neurosurgery and Psychiatry*, 41, 452–457.

Veltman, J.C., Brouwer, W.H., van Zomeren, A.H., & van Wolffelaar, P.C. (1996). Central executive aspects of attention in subacute severe and very severe closed head injury patients: Planning, inhibition, flexibility, and divided attention. *Neuropsychology*, 10, 357–367.

Vendrell, P., Junque, C., Pujol, J., Jurado, M.A., Molet, J., & Grafman, J. (1995). The role of prefrontal regions in the Stroop task. *Neuropsychologia*, *33*, 341–352.

Vercoulen, J.H.M.M., Bazelmans, E., Swanink, C.M.A., Galama, J.M.D., Fennis, J.F.M., van der Meer, J.W.M., & Bleijenberg, G. (1998). Evaluating neuropsychological impairment in chronic fatigue syndrome. *Journal of Clinical and Experimental Neuropsychology*, *20*, 144–156.

Vygotsky, L.S. (1962). *Thought and language* (E. Hanfmann & G. Vakar, Trans.). Cambridge, MA: MIT Press.

Vygotsky, L.S. (1978). *Mind in society*. Cambridge, MA: Harvard University Press.

Vygotsky, L.S. (1987). Thinking and speech. In L.S. Vygotsky, R.W. Rieber (Series Eds.), & A.S. Carton (Vol. Ed.), *The collected works of L. S. Vygotsky. Vol. 1: Problems in general psychology* (N. Minick, Trans.). New York: Plenum Press.

Ward, T. (1997a). *A neural network model of the central executive*. Paper presented to the Annual Conference of the British Psychological Society, Brighton, UK.

Ward, T. (1997b). A note of caution for clinicians using the Paced Auditory Serial Additions task (PASAT). *British Journal of Clinical Psychology*, *36*, 303–307.

Ward, T. (2002). *The University of the West Indies Cognitive Assessment System (UWICAS)–validation and norms*. Paper presented to the International Neuropsychological Society, Toronto, February 2002.

Ward, P.B., Catts, S.V., Fox, A.M., & Michie, P.T. (1991). Auditory selective attention and event-related potentials in schizophrenia. *British Journal of Psychiatry*, *158*, 534–539.

Weiler, M.D., Holmes Bernstein, J. Bellinger, D.C., & Waber, D.P. (2000). Processing speed in children with attention deficit/hyperactivity disorder, inattentive type. *Child Neuropsychology*, *6*, 218–234.

Weintraub, S., & Mesulam, M. (1987). Right cerebral dominance in spatial attention: Further evidence based upon ipsilateral neglect. *Archives of Neurology*, *44*, 621–625.

Weschler, D. (1955). *Weschler Adult intelligence Scale, manual*. New York: Psychological Corporation.

Wickens, C.D. (1984). Processing resources in attention. In R. Parasuraman & D.R. Davies (Eds.), *Varieties of attention*. London: Academic Press.

Wigal, S.B., Swanson, J.M., & Potkin, S.G. (1997). Lateralized attentional deficits in drug-free and medicated schizophrenic patients. *Neuropsychologia*, *35*, 1519–1525.

REFERENCES

Williams, G.V., & Goldman-Rakic, P.S. (1995). Modulation of memory fields by dopamine D1 receptors in prefrontal cortex. *Nature, 376,* 572–575.

Williams, M.A., LaMarche, J.A., Alexander, R.W., & Stanford, L.D. (1996). Serial 7s and alphabet backwards as brief measures of information processing speed. *Archives of Clinical Neuropsychology, 11,* 651–659.

Wilson, B., Alderman, N., Burgess, P., Emslie, H., & Evans, J. (1996). *Behavioural assessment of the dysexecutive syndrome.* Bury St Edmunds, UK: Thames Valley Test Publishing Company.

Wilson, B., Cockburn, J., & Baddeley, A. (1985). *The Rivermead Behavioural Memory test.* Bury St Edmunds, UK: Thames Valley Test Publishing Company.

Wilson, B., Cockburn, J., & Halligan, P. (1987). *The Behavioural Inattention test.* Bury St Edmunds, UK: Thames Valley Test Publishing Company.

Wilson, B.A., Evans, J.J., Emslie, H., Alderman, N., & Burgess, P. (1998). The development of an ecologically valid test for assessing patients with dysexecutive syndrome. *Neuropsychological Rehabilitation, 8,* 213–228.

Wilson, F.C., Manly, T., Coyle, D., & Robertson, I.H. (2000). The effect of contralesional limb activation training and sustained attention training for self-care programmes in unilateral spatial neglect. *Restorative Neurology and Neuroscience, 16,* 1–4.

Ylikoski, R., Ylikoski, A., Erkinjuntti, T., & Sulkava, R. (1993). White matter changes in healthy elderly persons correlate with attention and speed of mental processing. *Archives of Neurology, 50,* 818–824.

Index

fronto-temporal dementia 35, 120
functional magnetic resonance imaging (fMRI) 20, 82

"g" 111
general intelligence 115
generalization 146, 150, 154
Galvanic Skin Response (GSR) 8
general purpose 8
goal neglect 23, 104, 110

habituation 84
Halstead-Reitan neuropsychological test battery 67
hard drive 32
Hayling Sentence Completion task 125
head injury 65, 66, 68, 73, 82, 100, 106
and control processes 106
hemi-inattention syndrome 92
hidden layer 141
hidden units 141
human immuno-deficiency virus 77
hyper-attention 135
hypoglycemia 77

iconic store 11
identity priming 84
illness representation approach 79
imaging 39
implantation 162
impulsivity 109
individual differences 65, 111, 159

inhibition 90, 104, 105, 123, 124, 125, 126, 127, 160
inner voice / speech 101, 126
input layer 141
inspection time 77
intelligence test 111
intentionality 105
interacting attentional mechanisms theory 96
interference control 103
internal codes 19
internalized speech 110
internal representations 94
ipsilesional 94, 95
ischaemic vascular disease 121

language 3, 110, 153, 160
late selection 10
learning algorithms 38
left neglect 92
lesion 38, 47, 147
letter fluency 125
Lewy bodies 87
and brain regions 87
Lewy body dementia 87, 120, 161
limited capacity 7
line bi-section 95
localization of function 159
long term memory 32, 33, 138
Lottery Ticket task 73

malingering 77
manual dexterity 47, 68
Matrices task 76
memory 3, 68, 115, 116
memory clinics 117
mobile phone 19